Fighting Darkness
-Joanne Bolton-

Cover Image by: Mpilo Msweli
Published by: Lulu.com

First published by Lulu.com 2016

A big thank you goes out to Lawrence Richardson, my friend and editor, for all his hard work on this book, his encouragement, patience and enthusiasm. I also thank Eloise Nel for her patience, encouragement and financial support. To my parents, for putting up and dealing with my Depression and Bipolar Disorder, I owe the world. Gareth and Genevieve, you two are the best friends anyone could wish for and I thank God for you. Another thank you goes out to all who tried to help me throughout the years with an encouraging word, a hug or just a smile. Thank you Mpilo for taking my mental image and creating one on paper to give me an awesome front cover.

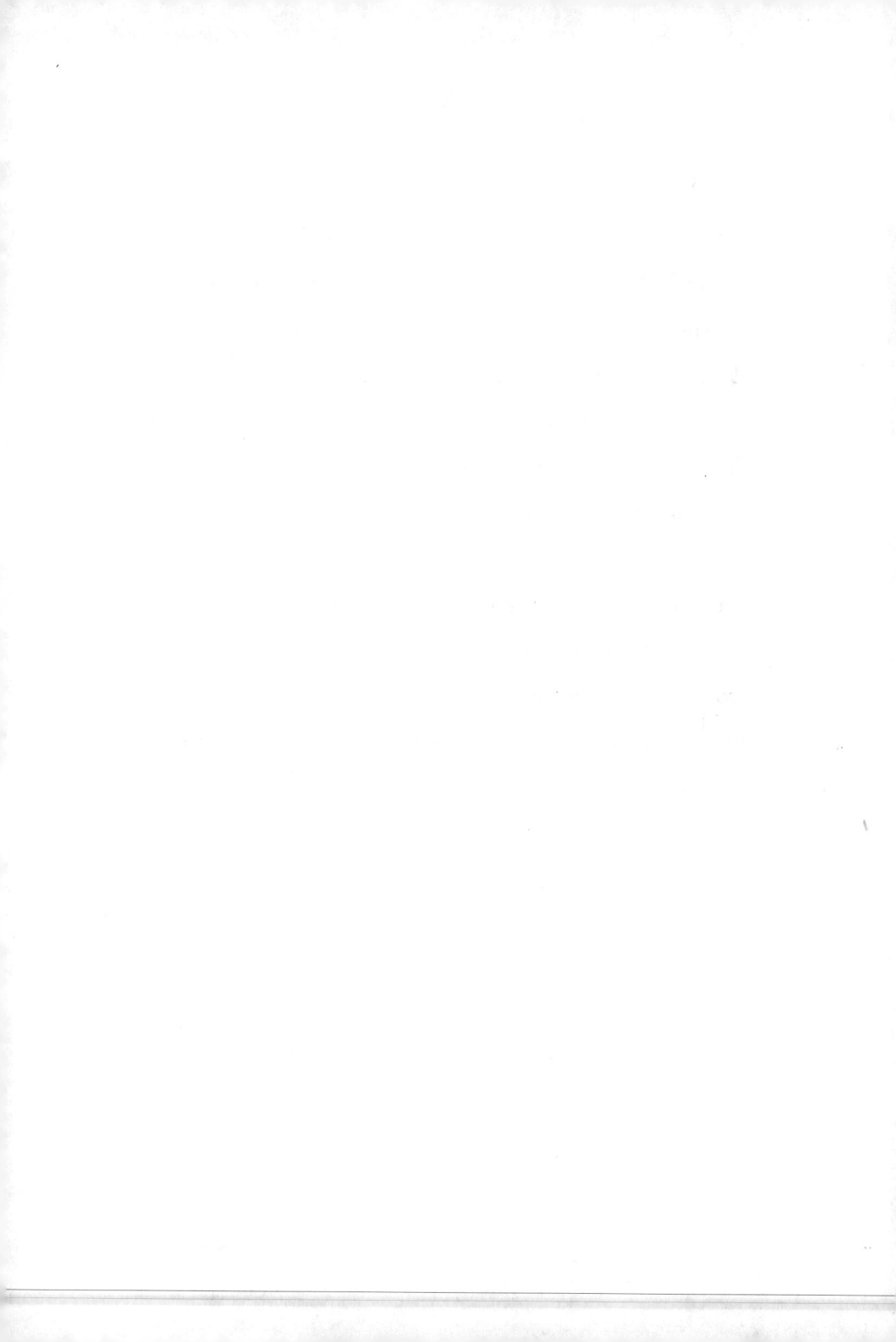

To all who have suffered and all who are still suffering

Alex loved the darkness that came when the sun rested and the moon rose. There were no judgemental eyes monitoring her every move and she was not followed by the frantic whispering and watchful gazes. She could hold her teddy and just be what she was: a little girl with darkness inside of her soul.

She was young, but she had learned to live behind a mask that hid her from the world. Nobody was allowed to see what she was feeling – they would not understand; for how could a four-year-old hate herself so much that she wished she could be anyone, or anything, else…that she wished she was dead and did not exist? No. Nobody could know. And so she hid behind a smile that never lit up her blue eyes with the sparkles that would have drawn people to her caring heart like a magnet picks up iron filings. Life was a masquerade – her paper face paraded for the world to see and believe within themselves that nothing was wrong with her heart, soul or spirit.

At dusk when the moon set her free, the smile faded into a stripe and the ability to talk dwindled to isolated silence. She no longer had to pretend to be normal – the same as every other child. Though tears soaked through her teddy's fur and snot trailed across her pillow she was free. She did not understand, but she was free.

If others had known about her pain and how deep it ran they would have only managed to confuse themselves by trying to figure out the cause. True, her family wasn't perfect and the fact that she was overweight annoyed her aunt and uncles to the extent that they ignored her attempts at affection and brushed her off like a pesky fly when she tried to be near them, but there was nothing traumatic that had happened to her. Her parents loved her, her baby brothers had been born that March and she loved them so much, and to the world her family was normal.

Inside she was far from normal. She knew she was loved, but was plagued by the thought that maybe she would say something that would make her parents push her away. Maybe the reactions of her aunts and uncles were the reactions that should happen to her. She tried her best to be the best. Never fail, never falter, never show a weakness or the inability to do something, never show fear...never admit to being anything other than normal.

She was full of questions but she felt that nobody was there to hear her ask them. So she set about inventing answers or trying to figure them out on her own. During the light she would smile and run and hang around the edges of groups pretending that she was a part of the conversation and that the birthdays they spoke about were parties she had attended, and that the luxurious things they owned were akin to the things that lay strewn around her bedroom for her to pick and choose from. She would laugh when they laughed, but only to appear the same. Oh, she got the jokes, but they were either crass or crap and not to her taste at all. Her opinions remained hers, because they just spoke over her if she said anything anyway, as what she had to say was never as interesting as any opinion they had. Her attempts at jokes belly-flopped painfully with the undignified splat of a toad falling into a puddle of mud each time they left her mouth, so she stopped trying.

She was the biggest of them all but the runt of the litter. Alex learned the art of being invisible and blending into a crowd to become one of the faceless that followed the leader. If she disagreed with them then she would turn and trudge to some secluded place of play and watch the group from a distance longing to be with them even as she watched them get into trouble for whatever it was they had done. They might have been trouble-makers, but they had friends.

Teachers knew their names and called on them in class to do tasks that she could have done if only given the opportunity. She faded into the background. Completing tasks and activities on time as perfect as she could make them, though perfect was never enough for her – there was always a fault, always something she could or should have done better.

Bathed and in bed, she could finally let out the breath she had been holding the entire day. That thing which differentiated her from all the other children, that darkness within, was free to roam her room with all its vicious energy fuming, flowing and firing foul shot after shot at her tiny heart. Her inner darkness would stand ruler straight like a Reverend and preach to her of all the things she wasn't and all that she could never be.

It would tell her that the reason the other children didn't like her was because of how fat she was, that was why they hated her. It would pontificate about her so called intelligence and how it made her stand out too much, making her a target for the muck that was thrown by children in their spiteful ways. Preach of how she was not up to the standard of the others. "Oh Alex, you'll never be as pretty as Olivia." "You can't even catch a ball; Johnny does that far better than you." "You call that a drawing? Well perhaps it might generously be called a copy…"

The sea of vitriol would wash her face as she listened to these sermons night after night – her darkness revealing the truth about her. The truth she could never let anyone see. She just wasn't good enough and never would be. So she would have to try harder…be better than her best, better than perfect. Second was not an option. The seas would crash against the rocks in her throat and break off crusty barnacles that burned as they were swallowed in drowning gulps. The darkness outside protected her, yet at the same time it allowed her demons free. Darkness followed her during the day and came out to bite at night.

Burrowing into her bed like an earthworm into his home she would hug Pinky to her with all her might and wish so hard that she just wouldn't wake up the next day. Perhaps, if she did, that she would be transformed into a normal little girl like her classmates, a normal little girl who liked pink lace and dresses rather than blue jeans and dirt. Who preferred to play with dolls instead of looking through books, skinny and beautiful like a princess with shining hair to match.

To her disappointment she always awoke, always herself; never transformed. Each day as she opened her eyes to the caress of the sun her darkness took up its position inside her heart and head, where it would spend all day whispering to her and poking holes in her heart. Maximising every fault and imperfection; overwhelming her with false facts of failure and that same imperfection.

Having to hide who you are is very tiring, because if your mask slips, even for a second, then everyone will find out just how much darkness is inside. Actors and actresses spend years of training and hard work to be able to pretend, they have all the things they need, props, wigs, costumes…things to remind them, but ultimately their mind has to be in the character. They have to become Sherlock Holmes – his essence, his spirit, his mindset and the way he looks at the world. They have to understand the complex emotions and circumstances that made the character. Their lives are dedicated to hiding themselves and becoming someone else for our entertainment.

Alex knew how to hide her darkness. How to smile and talk with a lilt in her voice that fooled everybody she came into contact with. To the world she was a happy little girl without a care in the world. Inside she was crumbs, dust, tumbleweeds and broken shards all guarded by an inexplicable darkness. She was four-years-old but she could have walked over any actress nominated for an Oscar without having had the years of study.

Even though her heart was being torn to shreds by this thing inside her, it was still a large heart capable of a large amount of love. She loved her two brothers with all her might and vowed that she would protect them with everything she had even if it meant her life. It shattered her when she accidentally dropped Peter when holding him one day. Her mother assured her it was an accident and that she wasn't in trouble, but she had hurt one of the very beings she had vowed to protect. She had failed at her task. She would not fail again. When her sister was born two years later Alex never asked to hold her out of fear of another failure. She helped with the bathing, gently sponging tickly toes and fidgety feet while Lauren giggled at the attention she was getting. Alex was a good foot washer and did her job diligently. She was also a good nappy changer. Lauren was well looked after, and Alex would let her fingers be played with and her hair nibbled as she leant over the cot. However she didn't dare hold her sister; she could not bear the thought of failing to protecting those that she loved again.

Karen Rivers watched her eldest child carefully, aware that something complex was happening behind those shuttered eyes. She did not know what it was, but she knew that there was something lurking in that young child's mind.

Alex started junior school the year she turned seven, by which time her short hair had grown down to her shoulder blades and her fringe would neatly tuck behind her ears leaving a middle parting that became a fashion to last her lifetime. Blue wire-frame glasses helped hide the blankness in her blue eyes, and also offered protection in the rare moments the mask slipped. Her teacher saw nothing wrong with the quiet, introverted little girl who worked hard without talking or causing disruptions. Alex coloured within the lines and never broke a rule, always had her homework done neatly and on time. While Mark sometimes caused trouble and got a ruler on his knuckles, Alex never invited any punishment, the punishment that went on inside was more than anyone else could give her.

After a short while the alphabet became something more than repetition of symbols, they became letters which became words which became sentences. Oh, the wonder of words! The worlds they unlocked and the places they took her. The library became her favourite classroom and she was overjoyed when she found out she could take books home to read as well. The friends she made bore strange names like Hansel or Snow White and each one lived happily ever after no matter how many times the story was told.

The class readers were classified according to difficulty of the book. The easiest readers were the "Kathy and Mark" series, while the hardest were those out of the dark blue box. Alex was in the top group for reading, the Apples. They were never referred to as the top group, but every child in that class knew that the Apples were the best at reading and were reading books that the Bananas and Cherries would probably only reach by the end of the year. Each day there was time set aside for the reading groups to come to the mat and read their homework from the previous day out loud.

One day Alex confidently read through a wonderful story about aliens and a fantastic female heroine who saved the day. She knew she had read well and that her pronunciation had been perfect even though some of the words were difficult. She had asked her parents the meanings of the difficult words and was ready to answer any questions Mrs Perkins asked her about the story. However, after she had finished reading there was an awkward silence. She closed her book and placed it on the ground in front of her and looked up – not exactly expecting praise or accolades, but maybe just a smile to show that she had done well. She was greeted with eyes like thunder and brows that melted into the wrinkled caused by the furious look on Mrs Perkin's face.

"Alex, where did you get that book?" Instead of her usual calm and kind voice icicles dripped from every word Mrs Perkins spoke and Alex began to feel them burning holes in her confidence as if they were coated in acid.

"From the light blue box Mrs Perkins."

"Look at the book Alex." Alex looked down at the book she had just completed reading. The cover was the same, a woman in a tight suit with a laser in her hand and her short hair blowing behind her as she stood on a platform. Alex looked up confused and helpless.

"Look at the book Alex." The fact that this statement had been repeated meant that there was something important that she was missing.

Something she had done was wrong. Sweat started its cold trickle down her hunched spine as she examined every inch of the cover on the floor in front of her. The pores at her hairline opened and began letting out panicked sweat. And then she saw it. Blinking did not make it disappear, it only brought it more into focus; a dark blue sticker. Something blocked her throat and Alex swallowed several times until she slowly lifted her head to meet the steel gaze of her teacher. She gulped, but the saliva stuck to the lump that was growing in her throat. Her hairline and spine felt icy as her cheeks burned with shame. She had a dark blue book.

"Where did you get that book from Alex?" Her voice was barely a whisper, but that whisper was sharp enough to pierce any form of self-control Alex had mustered.
"From the light blue box.."
"Is it a light blue book Alex?" Looking down into her lap Alex mumbled a quiet reply.
"I asked you a question Alex."

"No Mrs Perkins." Shame burned her face as nerves cooled her neck.

"Then why are you lying Alex?"

Alex looked at her lap again, shaking slightly. How could she explain to her teacher, an adult, an authority figure, someone she respected and admired that she was telling the truth without making Mrs Perkins seem like the liar? Blinking back tears of shame and confusion Alex looked up and mumbled a hoarse whisper that she was sorry.

Mrs Perkins nodded and Alex thought the incident was over but instead, the teacher, rose and went to the star chart that was stuck on the right of the blackboard. With her black marker she made a mark next to Alex's name. Alex's eyes felt as though they were glued to that mark, it stuck out like a rusty nail and shouted to the world that Alex Rivers had done something wrong. Not just something wrong, but something bad enough to earn herself a black mark. It shone darker than the

17

gold stars preceding it and Alex could not look away even as Mrs Perkins put down the marker and returned to her seat at the head of the semi-circle. Surely this was a bad dream and if she blinked hard enough that mark would not exist. Only the naughty children like Thomas and Claudia got black marks…what had she done wrong? The book had been in the light blue box… that was where she had gotten it from. She wanted to shout that she didn't deserve that mark on her record, she was not a liar, she had done nothing wrong, but while her heart beat the injustice throughout her body the darkness in her head laughed and cackled in glee. It stroked her neurotransmitters and drowned out the sound of her heart with its murmuring to her that she deserved all punishment.

Simon read, then Lucy, and then the remaining group members, but Alex did not hear a word. The black mark on the chart behind her burned its shameful gaze into her back and the darkness inside her gorged on that shame and confusion. Feelings overwhelmed her seven-year-old heart and she struggled to maintain control of the mask that simply had to be put into place. The darkness filled her head with thoughts of how bad she had been, how naughty, how shameful it was to get a black mark. Oh how she deserved it, disobedient and naughty child that she was. She deserved a whole row of black marks, a whole chart of shame just for herself.

Back at her desk, while the Bananas were reading, Alex let the mask slip for just a second as a solitary tear slid down her cheek, plunging from it to splatter a perfect circle upon her desk. She placed her sleeve over the drop and it vanished from sight. When she lifted her sleeve no physical evidence of that drop remained. The only proof that it had ever existed was the slight shake of Alex's hand as she reached for her pencil to complete her work and the memory of an acidic teardrop burning through her soul the way that black mark seemed to burn the chart with the evidence of her failure and shame.

Time is a tricky thing to measure. Sometimes one feels as if they have slept for hours but only five minutes have passed, and sometimes what feels like only five minutes sleep passes in two hours.

Most of Grade two was filled with reading new books, learning new words for spelling and working on more difficult subjects like Mathematics. Each year brought with it the Inter-House Athletics and Inter-House Gala events. To encourage healthy competition each child was placed in one of three 'houses' where, just like in Harry Potter, good behaviour and various other tasks earned you points. Each Monday in assembly the points were read out and there would be a winning house for the week. Alex was in Clear, their colour being white or blue, and there were also Wells (yellow) and Gardener (maroon or red).

Alex was overweight, something she had been all her life and something that caused her great pain as it was something she was desperately ashamed of. Perhaps it was this shame that made her start to hide away from everyone; perhaps it was the darkness, perhaps a combination of both. Whatever the reason, the darkness seemed to feed off the shame, pain and the humiliation that occurred came from each physical education lesson where everyone had to do an assortment of sports and exercises. Alex did not participate in the Inter-House Athletics. That was for the fit, strong and skinny. Those who could run fast and far and bring praise to their house. The whole school had to watch though, which was a nice break from work, but spending a whole day watching athletics was not entertaining at all. Each race was the same except for the distances.

The same was true for the Inter-House Gala, where the fastest and the best swimmers competed to win the trophy and shield that would bear their house's name for the rest of the year. Even though Alex did swimming, one had to do a summer and winter sport, she was more of a whale than a dolphin and once again took the place of a spectator.

Envy had been growing inside her, fed by the darkness that overflowed in joy at her pain. Why couldn't she run fast like Simone? Or swim like Claire? They won all their races and earned points and Clear house won both trophy and shield for many years. Alex had never picked up a magazine and admired the models in the fancy clothes that were currently being sold as perfection. She didn't need to; she simply looked at the children around her and wished with all her might that she could be like them. Happy, smiling, surrounded by friends, beautiful, smart and funny…loved. The darkness sewed envy into her heart with strings of jealousy and a needle of shame. No matter how hard she wished, she would never be like them.

In Grade three, when she was nine, Alex started piano lessons. Even before she had learned to play anything her grandfather had given her a piano stool that opened to hold her music and a brown leather satchel that fastened with a silver bar in the front. The satchel was once his, and for the first time in her life Alex felt as if she had done something right, that she had made them proud instead of being a disappointment. The more she learned about piano the more she enjoyed playing it, and according to her teacher she played it well with an excellent sense of rhythm and timing. But to her ears the notes sounded off-beat and the tiniest mistake rang out like the bells of Notre Dame announcing yet another failure. Even though her teacher told her to just keep playing if she made a mistake, few if any would know the difference, Alex knew the difference. She knew when she had failed to hit the right note, when the timing was off, and she was terrified of making a mistake. Each year there was a music concert where each music student would play a piece in front of family, friends and fellow students. No matter how well Alex knew the piece, she knew her hands shook as they hovered above the ivories and the fierce concentration creased her brow and stiffened her back. The smallest shake of her hand would play an extra note and shame would bloom on her cheeks as though someone was blowing on coals to heat them. After each performance she would repeatedly go through the piece in her head, analysing every single note she had played and reprimand herself for not playing it this way or that way. For playing it wrong, missing the timing, starting too slow, not playing the correct dynamics…and the darkness would rub its hands together as it fed upon the thoughts and nourished them until they completely consumed her mind. And as she listened to the other children play she wished she could play with their talent, their grace and poise.

The darkness completely hid the fact that she was just as talented as they were from her. In her mind she was inferior and could not compare to their awesomeness, and because she could never compare she was never ever going to be good enough or worthy enough.

Grade four passed much the same. New subjects were introduced and learned, some easier than others, but no matter what subjects she was good at Alex always noticed the ones that she struggled with. Afrikaans, Mathematics, writing in cursive...one mistake and her insides burned with shame at her failure to be perfect. Even if she got 99%, that elusive 1% would haunt her for days upon end. Jokingly her father would ask her what happened to that 1% and the darkness would rejoice at the feelings of failure that coursed through her body within the very blood that sustained her. She wasn't living up to her parents expectations, she was a failure as a daughter, she was not setting a good example for Peter, Adrian or Lauren to follow – she had to be the best so that they had a solid foundation to follow when the time came to begin their schooling.

Failure piled upon failure as one failure begat another which in turn bred yet more. The lost one per-cent became two, then three, then four, then ten as the content became harder and harder. She was still in the top group of her class but she was not the best. Her marks were not the highest, she never got close to one hundred per-cent and she burned with failure as test after test after test brought back results of fifteen out of twenty or eighty nine out of one hundred.

Pinky had been replaced by Charlie, and each night he was soaked until he had a salty core. Her father would sing her to sleep and turn out the light. As his footsteps receded down the passage the first wave would hit, she would bury her head in Charlie's neck and cry out to whoever might be listening to make her different. Take away this darkness. Make her a good girl that her parents could be proud of and that her family could love. Every morning when she woke she was the same person with the same feelings and the same problems. Darkness clutching her heart as a trophy while it sat enthroned within her mind and spewed its poison throughout her body. She would never…she could never…she wasn't….she didn't….she couldn't…

26

Darkness was all she knew. When she would receive
praise for anything it would confuse her, because she
had not done it perfectly. She didn't deserve the praise.
When she was told she had a gift or a talent she would
politely smile and nod but believe completely that they
were lying just to try and make conversation. Darkness
was her ruler, and its fists were spiked with iron.

One of her greatest struggles that plagued Alex was
writing in cursive. She could not get her brain and
hand to replicate the beautiful loops and twirls on the
board in front of her. She tried writing slower, but that
only caused incomplete work and the shame of that
burned worse than the ugliness of her handwriting.
Somehow words that she knew spelled themselves
differently when joined together by loops that should
have been graceful but which looked as undignified as
someone wearing jeans to a black-tie event. Her writing
exercises became full of underlined words – simple
words whose spelling she knew for sure until the letters

had to be joined together. Writing was something she had always loved, but as she struggled with cursive she began to loathe any writing activities, even if it was writing her name on a test page.

She gave up trying to make friends entirely. Nobody wanted to be associated with the fat kid, so nobody did and Alex didn't push herself upon anybody because the possibility of rejection was too fearful to contemplate. Books were her friends. Stories of lands that had lived in the imagination of authors until they had penned the words thus making the stories immortal and sharing their joys, triumphs, trials and tribulations with others. Characters came to life as fantastic descriptions made them leap off the page into her head. She saw their faces, the way they moved, the deeds they did. She heard their voices, the different accents and ways of speaking. Each character was a friend for the brief time they were with her, and the more she read the briefer the time became; she became a fast reader devouring books with a gluttonous appetite. They became a drug to her and as with all drugs she quickly needed more to achieve the escape she wanted from them. Soon one book wasn't enough. The thicker the book the better the story, but even the thick books could not last forever, she needed more and more to read before she could find that minute place of peace in her mind where the darkness was soothed to a brief rest by a good story.

As she got older the darkness grew stronger, filling her with loathing towards anything she did. No matter how many compliments or how much praise she received she believed everything she did to be worthless.

She knew she was different, inside and out. Inside was the darkness, which she felt nobody could ever understand, boiled and burned. On the outside her pale skin, that even the warmest sun could not turn golden brown, was stretched over layers of blubber.

Always hovering on the fringe, the very edge of the group, she longed to belong and be part of a group. She prayed she could have someone to talk to about normal things like books and television shows.

When she was eleven another overweight girl happened to be shuffled into Alex's class. While Emily was also overweight, she was the exact opposite of Alex. She was boisterous, extroverted, loud, charismatic and full of energy. She didn't seem to mind the way she looked, and instead of hanging around on the fringes of anything, she made sure her voice was heard within every conversation. Yet still the two girls were grouped as 'friends' due to their similar build.

Unfortunately Emily was not the greatest friend, Alex found out the hard way she could not share secrets with her because within a few moments the entire school would know the secret. So Alex carried on holding all the important stuff inside and learnt to perfect the art of polite, false conversation. Safe topics like television, weather and household pets were addressed while Alex's heart and mind remained trapped in the claws of the darkness, whirling in a pool of confusion and hurt. As the darkness grew she was more and more convinced that she could let nobody ever know the extent that it controlled her, the hold it had. After all who would understand? She would rationalise to herself. Her innermost, secret, thoughts and fears had to be contained, so she began sophisticating her internal filing system. Emotions went straight into boxes without letting any true feeling break through and thoughts were placed underneath layers of pretence then locked up deep within the tightest and most impenetrable vaults she could make. She did not talk – there was no way for her to express or release the toxic build up inside her head.

And then she discovered another side to words.

She had devoured books as if they were life-giving water since she had learned to read, but at age eleven she discovered that she could write words as well. Stories and poems that let out tiny pieces of her hidden secrets and helped her hold the burdens. Poetry came accidentally and it never left.

"Alright class," Mrs Edwards waited for some sort of general quiet before continuing, "this Friday is grandparent's day. As you know your grandparents will be visiting the school to see how well you work and there will be a special assembly." Her words passed over the heads of the class in waves of undisturbed air until she spoke the following. "For our grandparent's day activity we will be writing a poem about our grandparents." Panicked silence filled the room as each eye was suddenly riveted upon Mrs Edwards's face. Allowing the silence to permeate for a few more seconds, Mrs Edwards watched the class silently before explaining the task in more detail.

Alex wrote a poem, then another and another. They flowed onto the paper as though there were a magical connection between her pencil and her brain. The writing was a scrawl as she hurried to capture all the thoughts and phrasing chasing their tails within her head onto that sheet of paper – her mind working faster than her hand could place the words down. Eventually she placed her pencil down and looked at her work. She had three poems. Sneaking a glance at the students around her she noticed that they only had a couple of lines and many of their pencils were hovering over the pages like cats waiting at a mouse hole to pounce when there was a hint of movement.

"Why aren't you writing Alex?" Mrs Edward's voice made Alex jump slightly and panic ran cold down her spine and began tearing her hairline.
"I...I'm finished Mrs Edwards." All she could manage was a hoarse whisper as she looked down at the desk terrified of meeting her teacher's gaze in case it held anger or revealed that she had done something terrible.

"Let me see." The teachers voice was curt and to the point, blunt, disbelieving. Alex handed her pages to the teacher and waited for the berating. She waited for the inevitable proof that what she had was terrible and had to be re-done. That her concepts were wrong or that she had rushed the task and was in trouble. Like an elastic band being pulled tighter and tighter the silence stretched and on.
"Which one are you going to use?" Mrs Edward's voice was gentle and contained an element of surprise

which couldn't be hidden. Mutely Alex pointed to the second piece. Placing the paper back onto Alex's desk Mrs Edwards moved on to check the progress of the rest of the class as she murmured "Good choice Alex. Great work."

Alex's heartbeat slowly began to regulate. Why wasn't she in trouble? Why was Mrs Edwards shocked? What had she done wrong? Thoughts and possible outcomes whirled throughout her head as she copied out the second poem in her neatest writing onto the card provided, decorating it with some colour until she could not add any more in fear of ruining it further. Not satisfied with the effect or the words, she handed in the completed poem at the end of the lesson and prepared for first break.

"Alex, come here please." Mrs Edwards stopped her at the door and Alex knew within her heart that now the punishment would come. Gulping past the frogs that had suddenly appeared in her throat she turned and walked back to her teacher's desk.

"Yes Mrs Edwards?" Barely a whisper, Alex's whisper sounded like a shout in the silence of the room. Now whatever she had done wrong would be revealed and she would have to try and fix it as best as she could. She waited for her punishment to be handed to her and slowly wriggled her fingers.

"Your poems were excellent."

It took a few moments for the words to reach her brain and Alex blinked. Excellent? The darkness inside her roared with the laughter of a lion – she is just trying to make you feel better, trying to bolster your ego by telling you lies. Her mind whirled as the darkness took it for a joyride. Looking up from her clasped hands Alex met Mrs Edward's eyes in confusion.

"Your poems were excellent Alex." Mrs Edwards spoke firmly, knowledgably, purposefully and looked straight into Alex's eyes. "You have a talent with words. You can mould them and bend them into powerful and complex sentences that touch a person's heart and allow them to feel the emotion within them. Sentences that still make absolute sense when they are read." Alex just nodded. Why was Mrs Edwards lying to her? Her poems were pathetic. She wished she could tear them up and pretend they had never been written.

Mrs Edwards watched the silent girl in front of her, whose brow was wrinkled in confusion and disbelief even as she nodded in agreement. "You have a real talent with words Alex. Not many people could write what you wrote today. Go and enjoy your lunch." The teacher watched the confused pupil leave the class and for the first time her hazel eyes noticed the slump of the shoulders that seemed to be bearing a huge weight. Running her hands through her short hair she noticed the trudge of legs that seemed too heavy and weary to continue and the head bowed in defeat. Polishing her glasses Mrs Edwards sat staring at the empty doorway long after Alex had left. For the first time Alex's inner darkness was seen by another person – an intuitive and excellent teacher – and as Mrs Edwards replaced her glasses and made her way to the staffroom for a much needed cup of tea she made plans to speak with Alex's parents. She was convinced Alex suffered with depression and something told her that this suffering had been going on for years without anybody noticing.

After the meeting between Karen Rivers and Mrs Edwards, a meeting Alex was not privy to, she was sent to a child psychologist called Milse Beldant. Milse was probably a good psychologist, but there was something about her that made Alex uneasy. Nothing specific and perhaps it was only the darkness pulling her away from the psychologist in fear that it would be removed from the host it had inhabited since birth, but Alex could not trust Milse. She would attend sessions every week and sit there playing with the children's toys that were meant for children half Alex's age. All the while Milse spoke.

"The father is sitting on the couch."

Alex moved him to the kitchen area. "The father is cooking supper."

Alex moved each doll to a different place and each move was annotated in a flat voice that tested the limits of all the patience Alex possessed. She longed to take the dolls and shove them down Milse's throat just to get the woman to shut up, but she just continued mechanically moving them from place to place.

Then she tried painting.

"The red paint is on the paper." Milse wrote no notes and Alex spoke no words. Inside her head the darkness giggled as it relaxed back into its possessive state. This woman was no bother to it. In fact she could not even scratch the surface of Alex's mask that hid the darkness so well.

"The blue paint is being used as sky." Milse droned on and Alex suppressed the anger that flared up against this useless woman. Who cared if the blue paint was being used as the sky? The sky was blue. That's a given on most days. Why did this woman have to comment on every single thing that Alex did as if it was an Olympic event or a grand achievement? She was eleven dammit, not two, so why was this woman treating her like a child? She could read 'adult' books deemed appropriate by her mother, she could hold her own in a superficial conversation and she certainly did not have the mentality of a child.

Milse kept commentating every session, no matter what Alex did. Painting, playing with dolls...somehow Milse even managed to comment on Alex's actions during games of Uno. Anger towards this woman burned inside Alex and stiffened her shoulders, but her mouth would smile and her voice would be upbeat. The darkness took in all the anger and frustration as nourishment and nutrition and grew stronger. This psychologist was useless and was simply wasting money that the Rivers could not afford.

Guilt plagued Alex during every session. Surely there was something she was doing wrong and that was why these sessions were not working? She was costing her family money that they could not afford to part with, money that did not deserve to be spent on her and would be better off spent on food or other necessary things.

After a few months of sessions Karen was called in for a chat. Alex sat in the car while Milse and her mother spoke about her and could only imagine the horrible things that were being said about her. How she wasn't doing this right, how she was wasting the money, how bad she was. Karen came out of the meeting somewhat defeated and Alex forced back tears of shame – she had hurt her mother. The next week came and Alex stopped going to see Milse. The woman had not helped at all and the darkness puffed out its chest in triumph. It could not be beaten down or made to obey commands it didn't want to obey – it was in control and it would remain that way.

Mrs Edwards kept her eye on Alex that year, and watched the child put up with teasing and bullying that seemed to not affect her at all as she showed no outward signs – no tears or tantrums. But Mrs Edwards knew that inside Alex was suffering and she wished there was something she could do to help the child. But nobody could help Alex until she realised that she needed help.

Karen sat on the edge of her bed with her head in her hands. Her freshly permed hair sprung like dirty-blonde twisty noodles from her head and the glasses that usually covered her blue eyes lay discarded on the bed beside her as long nails gripped her forehead in an attempt to keep her thoughts in order.

A few rooms over Alex lay in bed, her hair, now shorter, splayed across the pillow like a Chinese fan. Blue eyes fixed on a speck of dirt on her ceiling she nibbled on nails already bitten to the core. Tasting blood, she finally put her hands down and rolled over to face the wall – her back to the world. Hugging Charlie tightly she wondered if it was normal for a thirteen-year-old to still have a teddy bear, but then she knew without a doubt that she was not normal. Eventually her eyelids dropped like stones and her subconscious filled her head with twisted tales where every failure was magnified and every embarrassment put on public display. Her face creased in her sleep and she shivered slightly. Even in sleep she was not at rest.

Alex had loved Irish music ever since she had borrowed a Dubliners CD from her mother's collection many years earlier. That year a troop of dancers from Lord of the Dance were touring South Africa. She knew that she would never be able to go – money was tighter than it had ever been. Her parents had seen the show a few years before when they had first been there on tour, and Alex had watched the video over and over again until the beats and taps were ingrained into her soul.

Grant Rivers went into Alex's room and placed a piece of paper on her desk where she was working. Glancing at the paper it took a while to register that it was a ticket. And not just any ticket, but a ticket to Lord of the Dance, an exceptionally rare and greatly treasured father-daughter treat.

Sitting in the theatre surrounded by people who understood and loved the magic of the show as much as she did was an experience she would never forget. The urge to clap and cheer after every number was an urge that filled the heart of every soul in the room. The music, dancing and lights that continued playing in her memory that night cast a magical spell over her as she slept. The fiddles, the group numbers, each perfect and uplifting. The sequence called "Siamsa" with its colours and rhythm variations, the violin duets that harmonised perfectly to bring across the most perfect sound enchanted her. The interaction between the 'good' and the 'bad' until good ultimately triumphed as it always does in stories... all of this left the darkness bewildered; it could not grab hold of her that night, and it lost its grip at times during the days that followed when the show was relived again in her mind. She would listen to the CD and watch the video and just let the music and the story filter through her until it had her absolute concentration. In those brief moments her mind was still, the darkness was

45

quiescent and her heart light. The music soothed and healed in a way that Alex could not begin to understand let alone describe. Soon she began collecting songs from various artists. No artist was her favourite, her tastes stuck to no genre. She simply picked songs that spoke to her heart with their lyrics or melodies. Music gave her rare moments of tranquillity as the darkness was suppressed by the tunes that made her tap her foot or bounce her head and she was lulled by lyrics that had been carefully thought out by the lyricist to evoke a particular feeling or tell a particular story. Music became her saviour. It did not always work, many times the darkness was stronger than the melody and not even the words could contain it, but the music swirling around her gave her a slight ability to live with the darkness. She didn't understand it, though it knew her all too well, but the music helped her hold it and keep it still.

Karen watched her daughter and saw the talents she possessed; the writing, the creativity, the ability to absorb words and their meanings through the books she read. The ability to copy images in front of her onto a piece of paper when drawing. Desperate to help free her daughter from the darkness, Karen turned to art therapy.

Each week Alex would visit Theresa and just create. She could paint, draw and work with clay or any combination of all of them. Theresa watched in silence as Alex worked, and even though there was still no pride in her work or the ability to acknowledge when she had done something well, Alex felt relaxed. The darkness would poke at her self-esteem from time to time, but it mainly left her alone because no therapy was happening. There was just art and an escape from a busy house with siblings who could grate nerves that never seemed to exist before they were grated.

It was with a smiling face and a sobbing heart that Alex said goodbye to Theresa after the final session. Karen had cancelled them because they weren't helping her daughter in any way except getting her out of the house. Oh how the darkness crowed in triumph at its invincibility, and its powerful grasp withered Alex's heart a little bit more. She was a failure at therapy. No words would come from her mouth or brain no matter how many times they circled her mind. Nobody will understand, the darkness told her maliciously. They will think you are a freak, abnormal, ugly, rotten inside… they will know just how much of a bad person you really are. And so Alex did not open her mouth during therapy; how could she trust someone who didn't know her when she couldn't trust those who did?

The year passed and with it came the Valentines Ball. Alex did not have a valentine, nobody gave her a second glance because of how ugly she was, but she went anyway because Emily was going. It was mortifying. The popular girls, all surrounded by their dates, bribed one of the boys in the class to dance with Alex. They stood an arm-length apart holding each other on the shoulders, the shoes she was wearing augmented Alex's natural height. The music was loud, but the sniggers were louder. The giggles of the popular girls as they watched the freak dance seemed to bounce and echo throughout the hall as if they were standing in a cavern or cave, and it was with relief to both parties when the song ended and they could remove their fingertips from each other's shoulders, mumble something polite and walk away.

The embarrassment of that dance haunted her for most of the year as the popular girls took delight in sniggering and pointing before breaking off into peals of laughter seemingly loud enough to permeate the entire school. Why could nobody love her? Why couldn't she be like Lucy, who had a boyfriend who would hold her hand and sit with her at break? Why couldn't she be like Sarah who had two boys fighting over her just to get her attention? No boy thought of her as anything except someone to play hand-tennis or hockey with. Her heart longed to be loved, to feel loved and to have someone to love. She knew she had love to give, but the darkness kept reminding her that nobody would or could ever love her so what was the point.

"Don't bother looking at your heart, nobody wants it" The darkness would whisper "forget about the love you have inside, just get through the day without being hurt". No matter how much the inside was dying She felt that she had to just carry on without letting the hurt show on the outside.

The year ended similar to the way it began, quietly. Alex attended the year-end function, as she was going into high school the following year, and went through the motions of pretending that she would miss her classmates who were moving off to different schools. She wished them well and smiled around at everybody portraying the same false excitement and happiness she used when she spoke with them. The darkness inside, bubbled over with unsuppressed power. It now had a whole new environment in which to thrive, new ways to prove to Alex that she was worthless and simply nothing. New people that would surround her yet never become her friends, new things to learn and understand which would present new opportunities to prove again and again just how big a failure she was. She was petrified. Elephants lived in her stomach never mind butterflies, but she smiled her spark-less smile and forced fake excitement into her voice as she spoke about a possible future. What future was there for her, for the failure that she was? She could not picture a future, could barely get through each hour of each day, but she spoke boldly about perhaps becoming a veterinary surgeon or maybe a journalist. Hollow lies, empty words and false smiles forced out from her mask while the darkness stroked her spine and whispered to her what a coward she was.

Mrs Edwards gave Alex an extra long goodbye hug when the time came for the students to say goodbye. She knew that the depression would only become worse, but she knew that there was nothing she could do. She had tried her best to get help for Alex. She had, however, succeeded in making Karen and Grant aware that their daughter was suffering daily. Mrs Edwards could only hope that this awareness would aid them in helping Alex towards her future. She knew that if Alex did not get the help she desperately needed she would not survive. Alex was already half-dead inside, emotions rotting in boxes and cabinets strewn throughout her brain where she had filed them in order to survive, where the darkness loved digging through the toxic waste to find another morsel to taunt her with. If she didn't get help soon she would die on the outside as well becoming just another suicide statistic, lost within the mathematical calculations and speculations.

Recommended by friends, the Rivers joined the Oakwood Baptist Church, and by mid-year Karen, Grant and Alex were baptised members. Peter, Adrian and Lauren weren't interested at all, and so the prayers for their immortal souls began in earnest. Alex was determined to prove that she could be a good Christian. Every day she read her Bible and prayed for her siblings and those around her. Instead of Sunday school, for smaller children, Alex attended Junior Bible Class which was for grade eights and nines. One of the leaders was particularly kind and emanated an air of trustworthiness.

Alex was still cautious so she observed Melissa Downs as subtly as she could. Melissa smiled a lot and the smiles were genuine. Her eyes had this unique ability to fill with genuine concern, understanding and love when talking to a person – making them feel as if she was entirely focused on them and what they were saying. Melissa had kind eyes, and was always generous with a comforting hug.

Slowly Alex began to trust Melissa, but not with the things buried so deep within her. She never mentioned the darkness, raising only superficial problems like how she was teased or how her brother had angered her. Melissa would sit and listen, eyes free from judgement or harshness, and Alex felt that maybe, just maybe, she had a friend she could depend on.

Apparently high school teachers are far more intuitive than junior school teachers, because she wasn't even half-way through grade eight when one of the teachers called Karen and Alex to a meeting where she announced that Alex was suffering from Depression and needed to see a psychologist. The darkness roared in fear, it had been named, but then settled down with a satisfied plop as Alex refused to believe a word. Depression was something that crazy people had. She was not crazy. She was worthless, ugly and a failure…but she was not crazy. Still, Karen nodded and

Alex found herself amazed that her own mother believed the nonsense being aired.

"I've noticed it for a while." Alex looked at her mother with horror gripping her, paralysing her, shaking her. Her mother thought she was crazy? "I always used to find blocks of cheese and jars of peanut butter in her cupboard when she was smaller," Karen continued, "I knew that she was comfort eating."

Comfort eating? Nonsense. Alex just liked cheese and why should she bother with bread when one can spoon the peanut butter straight from the jar? Her hands began to slowly curl into fists as she listened to the conversation floating around her.

"Her grade five teacher also noticed, so we went to a child psychologist. I don't know if you know her, Milse Beldant?"

"I have heard of her, apparently she is really good, but I think that perhaps Alex was too old to be a patient of Milse's."

"Yes, she was. They didn't get along. Milse just frustrated Alex and I stopped the sessions because they weren't helping. I did try art therapy, but Alex just used that as an escape from home and a time to do art, there was no therapy happening. I stopped that too."

Fingers curled tight and hands shaking Alex looked at a spot on the wall. She refused to look at her mother. Her mother thought she was crazy, thought that she needed 'psychological help'…thought she was Depressed? No! She was not depressed and she never would be. She was just an ugly worthless failure without friends who isolated herself and was very introverted. Depression? No! Never! She didn't need people, she had books. She didn't need to talk, she could write. She didn't need any psychological help – she was fine. She liked reading better than having worthless conversations about superficial topics with superficial people who only cared about boys and clothes and things that Alex could never hope to afford. She was not depressed.

"I recommend Beverly Green. Her office is at Oakwood General Hospital, just down the road. She is very good." Karen nodded and took down the details offered to her before standing and shaking hands with the observant teacher. Alex forced her hands to go limp, rearranged her face to a neutral expression and politely said goodbye. A feeling of dislike and exceptional fear towards Mrs Black was planted inside Alex's heart that day as the darkness panicked. It would not be named, it would not be vanquished. Alex belonged to it and it would never let her go, so Mrs Black was a threat from that day forward. An extra bright smile would curl the corners of Alex's lips when she passed Mrs Black in the corridor and her greeting would be chirpy and airy – full of light.

Karen took her daughter to Beverly Green. Sitting in the office they filled out the patient information form with all the necessary boring details. When the form was handed to the receptionist, they sat back waiting.

Alex fidgeted, her thumbs rolling over one another subconsciously. She stared at the strategically placed pamphlets, there to catch the eye. She noted the details of the room, it's TV precariously balanced on rickety brackets, the doors, the windows, The TV drone from its corner about nothing that interested her, the particular wear of the well-trodden carpet. The way the office was shared with a gynaecologist so most of the pamphlets were related to pregnancy issues and information and could be ignored.

The door beside Alex popped open like a hatch in a machine and a man stepped out accompanied by a short, round woman wearing black-rimmed glasses.

"Thank you so much Beverly." He grasped the woman's hand, shaking it with a smart motion. "Thank you for your help. I'll see you next week."

The man made his way over to the receptionist to book another appointment while Alex watched the little round woman scanned through the forms that her mother had completed, what felt like so many years ago. Finally a piercing, hard and demanding green gaze was directed at Alex and a hand over-decked in gaudy rings ruffled messy curls.
"Follow me Alexandra Rivers." Ordered the woman. With a nod and her insides shaking like electrified jelly Alex got up and walked slowly through the door that had been beside her, into the room she'd seen this woman and the handshaking man come out of.

As Beverly shut the door the gloom inside seemed to intensify, even though the blinds were open and sunlight hit various objects on the desk.

"Have a seat." The woman indicated a chair on one side of the desk while she made her way to one on the other side. She surveyed the girl for a moment, and Alex forced herself to appear calm and in control. She would not show fear, she would not show nerves…she would prove that she was normal and did not need to be here.

"So, you are Alexandra Rivers." Again Alex nodded then pulled a tissue from the box in front of her. Slowly she began to shred it into the smallest pieces she could.

"What brings you here today Alexandra?"

"My mother seems to think I need to be here." The tissue was getting smaller and a large pile of fluffy white shards was filling Alex's lap.

"And you disagree?" Another nod from Alex as Beverly noted something down on the pad of paper in front of her before looking up again.

"Why does your mother think you need to be here Alexandra?" Alex shrugged and continued shredding.

She dared to peek at the woman observing her, but green-mamba eyes quelled any ability to speak. This woman would not understand what Alex could not explain. She was not depressed, she only had darkness. She was just bad and a failure and simply needed to try harder. Her blue eyes took on a grey hue as she took another tissue from the box and began to add to the pile of fluff in her lap.

"How are you feeling Alexandra?" Beverly began to tap her pen on her pad of paper out of irritation. Alex dared not say a word. Feeling? She felt nothing that was good or worth sharing. All her feelings were bad – sadness, anger, hurt. She couldn't talk about those, it wasn't allowed. She began to twist the shards of tissue in her lap as the tapping of the pen grew louder in the silence until it seemed to echo around the room.

"Tell me about yourself Alexandra."

"I'm thirteen." Alex mumbled

Beverly made another note then looked up. Alex's eyes stayed fixed on the pile of tissue on her lap as if it could teleport her somewhere else, anywhere else.

"Do you enjoy school Alexandra?" Beverly questioned and Alex nodded whilst another note was added to the sparse page.

After what felt like an eternity of torture in hell Beverly finally announced that the time was up. Alex stood up gratefully, sweeping the tissue crumbs into the bin, and followed Beverly from the room. The round woman walked briskly as if she was impatient to get somewhere, and after placing Alex's folder down at reception her venomous eyes looked at Alex, but it was to Karen that she spoke.

"Alex is not depressed Mrs Rivers." Something tight in Alex's chest loosened a little bit. "She is merely uncommunicative."
"But if you just spoke…"

"She is uncommunicative Mrs Rivers," Beverly cut Karen off mid sentence, "and that's all there is to it. She doesn't need to see a psychologist, she needs to get her act together and just interact more with the people around her." Glaring at Alex for wasting time that could have been used to help someone who really needed help, she turned back to the desk...conversation over. She picked up another folder, called another name and walked back into the office to see to another shaking patient...someone she considered a proper patient by the look of him.

Karen watched her daughter silently. There was no outward change in her demeanour from before she had entered the room. She still stood with her head down and her hands in her pockets, hunched over. Karen knew that Beverly was wrong, but she did not know what to do. The psychologist would not listen to her. Sighing quietly to herself she began to leave the office with Alex trailing along behind her.

Inside Alex the darkness chuckled to itself, it had fooled that idiot of a psychologist. Once more it took up a firm stance within Alex and resumed feeding her the lies it had fed her since as far back as she could remember. Alex simply listened to the words floating in her head. They wanted her to interact? Fine, she would interact, she had done it before – pretended to be part of a group that didn't want her around, it was nothing new to her and she knew that performance well enough. She would simply have to try harder to make it appear as if she was actually a part of the group. Laugh more when a stupid joke was told even though it was far from funny. Plaster a smile upon her face until cracks appeared from the effort, and then plaster upon the plaster. Her mask would have to be thicker than ever. Nobody could see inside her, see how weak and pathetic she was. She had to be strong and perfect. She knew she had already failed at being a beautiful girl, failed at being worthy of love, failed at being top of the class... She couldn't permit any more failure. Depressed? Her? Never! She was not crazy.

Hiding herself during the day was exhausting, yet Alex could not sleep at night. She would lie awake as the day's events would circle her head in cyclones of repetitive self-doubt. She would pick out moments where she could have tried harder, should have been better, could have done this or should not have done that. She would plan for the next day; if this happened this is what she could do, or if someone said this then that is what she might say in response. She examined the next day from every angle she could think of and tried to plan a way to get through it.

She felt her mask was weighing her down and her heart had been hollowed out and filled only with pain. Nobody could see the pain, nobody knew the pain…how do you explain a pain that shouldn't exist? There was no medical condition – it was not as if she had a broken bone in a cast which was supposed to hurt. She just had the darkness as her companion and a body filled with hurt that came without reason to overwhelm her and cover her like a wet blanket smothering the passionate fire that her talents could have brought out of her. She hated herself for being who she was; worthless, a failure, a freak, ugly, a burden, a bad example…but mostly she hated herself for feeling this pain that should not be there. It would come bubbling up like acid reflux and burn through the walls around her heart until it was burning her heart itself. With the pain came other feelings that could not be identified, and there was never a reason for them. They just came at random moments and would not go away. So Alex began writing.

Poem after poem flowed from her pen as emotions soaked into simple paper and the pressure was relieved just a little bit. Eventually she gathered her courage and showed one of these poems to Melissa, who read it with eyes that showed concern but never lost their kindness. From then on that was how she spoke. She would write poetry and show some of it to Melissa who would either talk through it or just be there.

By the time she was fourteen the darkness was her and would bring up feelings daily that had no reason to be there. Writing, while it helped, was not enough to express the pain – to make it real. One day Alex picked up a box cutter and took the blade out. She ran the blade over the top of her foot and a thin line of read appeared. She did it again and again until a whole neat row of lines marked her foot. As each tiny red beaded line appeared her soul began to breathe and the pain evaporated. Alex hid the blade and put on a pair of socks. Her foot hurt, but it had a reason to hurt – it was bleeding from cuts. Her heart was uneasy, but the pain was gone. Pain had replaced pain, the physical replaced the emotional and she felt, for a time, she could breathe again.

Alex continued releasing her pain through poetry, and when everything was just too much out would come the blade and another line would be added to her foot – her heart, finally, breathing through scarlet stripes.

Although the pain eased things she soon needed more, deeper and harder, longer and wider stripes of crimson until one day Alex took a kitchen knife and stabbed it into her leg. It made an odd popping sound as it entered, much the way it sounds when you stab a piece of raw meat with a knife. She simply looked at the red handle sticking out of her body. There was no pain at all, so she pulled out the knife, washed it off and carried on with her day.

Beth was a year ahead of Alex in school, but they went to the same church and so sometimes Alex and Beth would chat during break. Each had their own 'group' to which they 'belonged' but they were also both part of one of the music bands. Waiting for practice one day Alex hoisted herself onto a ledge and the skirt of her uniform lifted slightly showing the thick white wound-worm from the healed stab wound. She brushed down her skirt to cover her leg and continued with the light conversation that they had been having, as if nothing happened. Beth, however, was observant.

"Where did you get that scar?"
"What scar?" Alex feigned innocence as her heart pumped panic into a brain frantically scrambling for some excuse, some reason for the scar.
"The one on your leg." She said blandly
"Cat scratched me." She knew the answer was lame but as it was the only thing that came into her mind, Alex spoke the words.
"Your cat has thick claws." Beth said mildly, betraying her disbelief as she looked Alex in the eye and Alex squirmed under the gaze.
"Maybe it was when I caught myself on the gate the other day." Alex tried but Beth just continued looking.
"Or maybe where I walked into that piece of metal we have around our Aviary at home." She lied again but was beginning to run out of ideas. Cocking her head to one side Beth said nothing. She simply looked at Alex.
"Show me." She demanded

Alex looked around for an escape route but there was none. Frozen to the ledge she felt as if the world was spinning out of control around her. Nobody was supposed to know! She had hidden it so well, and now she had made a mistake and Beth had seen. What could she do? How could she escape?

"Show me." Beth demanded again, not letting Alex forget. Alex pushed herself up on her arms a little, ready to hop off the ledge, but Beth placed her hands over Alex's and forced her back down.

"Show me." She ordered a third time. So Alex did. The neat rows of white lines jumbled with fresher red ones that covered her foot, the three or four worms that lived on her legs and the single mark on her arm that had been passed off as a scratch from the gate a few months before. Beth said nothing, the rest of the group arrived and practice began. She stole glances at Beth from time to time, but her friend seemed to have put the incident behind her and was focussing on the practice. Alex copied, hoping that it was an end to the issue.

The next day, perched on another ledge in the shade by the stairs, Alex became aware of two figures standing in front of her. She lowered whatever book she happened to be reading that time and nodded a greeting to them. Nancy was in Alex's year, but had become Beth's shadow.

"I've made an appointment for you to see Ms Carmichael tomorrow at second break." Beth announced firmly.
"I'm not going." Alex replied just as firmly
"You either go see Ms Carmichael or you go see Mrs Black, and I know how you feel about Mrs Black." Beth had Alex cornered.
"Why does she need to go see Ms Carmichael?" Nancy chirped. Alex began to panic. She was cornered with no escape. Beth knew, obviously Ms Carmichael knew

71

because Beth would have had to tell her why she was making the appointment. Now Nancy was curious, and if she didn't go see Ms Carmichael then Mrs Black would know and then who knew who else would know her secret. The darkness inside her flooded her with fear – she had been found out – and she had the strongest urge to simply drop everything and run as far away as she could get.

"Tomorrow. Second break." Beth ordered as she folded her arms, making it known that she would brook no argument.

"I can't…" Alex tried

"Then I'm calling Mrs Black, and she just walked past the door." Beth cut her friend off and began to climb the stairs.

"No!" Alex called out, Beth turned. "I'll go, but you come with me." Alex could only whisper in shame. Nancy looked from Beth to Alex, somewhat clueless yet somehow knowing at the same time.

"Have you been hurting yourself?" She suddenly blurted out the words like projectile vomit. Alex looked around to see if anyone had heard, but there was nobody else there so she nodded her reply. "You shouldn't do that. It's not good you know. You could get blood poisoning and die." Nancy announced dramatically.

God please let me get blood poisoning and die before tomorrow, Alex prayed, as she watched Beth pull Nancy to one side and harshly chide her. Her darkness was laughing while she was shaking in fear. Nobody would understand this. They could not understand that it was the only way that she could let go of the pain that came out of nowhere and just breathe, just survive. Everyone would think she was doing it for attention, to draw people towards her in hope of making new friends or influencing them. The darkness fed her mind with thoughts of how the meeting could go – what would be said, how it could go wrong, what would Ms Carmichael think about her, what did Beth and Nancy think about her. She couldn't breathe and the darkness twirled her mind in a dizzying dance of defiance against any preparations she could try to make before the meeting.

Fear was the very marrow of her bones and her hands shook as she picked up her book again. Concentration escaped her and she found herself staring at the letters as if she had never seen them before. Oh God what would happen tomorrow? Nobody was supposed to know how bad of a person she was, how worthless and pathetic. Now Beth and Nancy and Ms Carmichael knew…and the knowledge that her darkness had pushed itself into her external world to affect her interactions with those three people scared her more than anything in the world. Would Beth desert her, leave her alone with the scars because she knew about them? Would Ms Carmichael tell the other teachers? Would they look at her differently? She tried her best to be the best student she could be, to respect, listen and do as she was told – would their opinion of her change if they knew this terrible thing about her?

The words on the page were still just a jumble of black symbols and Nancy and Beth were still arguing a few meters away. How could she explain this? Would Ms Carmichael understand that she was not seeking attention? That she desperately wanted to hide it – to hide the cuts and the pain they revealed... the darkness that was intruding into her physical life. What if Ms Carmichael wanted to tell her parents... would her mom and dad understand? Would they hate her for the failure that she was or would they recognise that she was fragile and be gentle with her? Would they understand this darkness that was now part of her and had been in her since she was a child? Would they be angry at her for causing problems? For attention seeking? – would they understand she wasn't seeking attention? What would they think of her? Would they still love her?

She took a gulp as the bell rang to signal the end of break. Would her parents understand that she was merely allowing her heart to release some pain so she could breathe? That it was the only way she could figure out how to survive each day? Would they know how hard it was to speak about all the pain and everything else lurking in the darkness? Would they understand that she had to let her blood speak for her?

A single tear dripped from the tip of her nose as she bent to put her book back in her bag.

If her parents found out... would they still love her?

No matter how afraid she was or how much she was hurting, Alex kept her promises. So at second break the next day she was standing with Beth outside the office Ms Carmichael shared with the other counsellor Mr Roberts. Alex felt like liquid trying to lean against the wall. Her heart sank somewhat as she saw Ms Carmichael approach along the passage– she had hoped that the counsellor would forget the appointment and things could go on as normal, she had hoped that anything might happen rather than have to face her. Beth gently squeezed Alex's elbow, but even though it was a gesture offering comfort, strength and support all Alex felt was terror. She prayed that the wall would swallow her, that Ms Carmichael would suddenly remember an urgent appointment, that there would be an alien invasion... but nothing happened. Glancing out of the corner of her eye at Beth standing beside her, Alex could not help but feel betrayed. The darkness inside longed to turn and shout out obscenities – how Beth had betrayed her trust, how she was only causing problems by interfering, how all Alex wanted was to be left alone with the darkness that was her companion. All the while, she wanted to thank her friend for caring enough to do something.

There was so much conflict going on within her regarding Beth that Alex didn't notice that Ms Carmichael had reached the office and unlocked the door. It was a gentle tug on her elbow that propelled her into the room and the click of the key in the lock that froze her in place so firmly that Beth had to drag her to the couch in the corner. Alex collapsed onto the floor while Beth sat on the couch. Ales sat with her legs crossed her balled fists in her lap and her head down. Beth picked up a magazine, a Cosmopolitan of all things, and began paging through.

"Hi, I'm Ms Carmichael." There was a weird energy emanating from the counsellor. A sense of understanding, acceptance, the want to help and a quirky personality all rolled into one. "You're

Alexandra Rivers. Grade nine D. You will be fourteen in a month or so." She stated more than asked but Alex nodded her agreement rather than trusting her voice.

"She prefers Alex." Beth interjected before returning to the magazine.

"So, Alex, Beth has told me a bit about you," Alex's hands clenched tighter, "but I would like to hear more from you." There was silence. The type of silence that is so silent it is deafeningly loud. "Well, let's start small. Tell me about your family." The councillor tried. Alex blinked; she knew she could do that.

"I have two brothers and a sister, Peter, Adrian and Lauren. The boys are twins. My parents are still married, been married almost 16 years. Their names are Grant and Karen." Alex spoke haltingly, unsure what this person was looking for from her. The counsellor took no notes. She simply slipped her shoes off and tucked her legs in a curl underneath her. "I have dogs. And cats. I like animals." Alex added as an afterthought, feeling that she had run out of words

"I've seen you reading." Ms Carmichael mentioned, gently encouraging Alex to continue.

"Yes. I like reading." Her answer was short and her voice quiet.

"Books help you escape this world don't they? They take you to a place where you can forget everything that's happening and just be somebody else. A place where you can meet people who will never abandon you." The councillor commented as Alex looked down again while her spine began to tingle with paralysis.

"Have you ever read anything by Marion Zimmer Bradley?" Ms Carmichael asked making Alex look up at the sudden change in direction.

"Never heard of her." Alex shook her head and mumbled.

"She has a series written around King Arthur and the mysterious island of Avalon. Good books. Remind me to lend them to you." Alex nodded, swallowed then nodded again.

"Now Beth tells me you've been hurting yourself."
Once more Alex looked down at her lap, her breathing
shallow and fast as her chest clenched with fear.
"Would you show me where?"

For a moment Alex froze, her mind a mess. She
mustn't see, she mustn't know… The darkness sang in
her head, Alex should just bluff, pretend she had no
marks. She closed her eyes in confusion and clenched
her fists so tightly that her shoulders shook.

Mouth set in a thin line and teeth grinding against each
other she slowly slid the skirt of her uniform up to
show the four lonely marks on her legs. Then she took
off her shoe and sock and showed the marks on her
foot. Finally she rolled up the sleeve of her jersey and
showed the mark on her arm. Exhausted and expecting
the worst she braced herself for what was coming.
How much trouble was she going to be in?

"What do you use?" Ms Carmichael asked in a gentle tone. Alex blinked at the unexpected question. "A box cutter blade or scissors." She murmured haltingly. "You should have a tetanus injection." Ms Carmichael absentmindedly mentioned. Alex was still focused on one of the checks in the skirt of her uniform. She didn't dare meet the counsellor's eyes.

The bell rang and Alex was at the door waiting to be let out before Beth had even managed to close the magazine.
"I'll see you tomorrow at second break," Ms Carmichael smiled as she unlocked the door. Outside Alex was met with the curious stares of students who wondered what she had done to need to see the counsellor. Alex merely nodded and slipped into the stream of students heading towards their various classes.

That night poetry could not help Alex cope and so the blade was brought out. Another cut on the leg. She felt she couldn't cut her arms, it was summer and she knew it would be difficult to explain a jersey in summer.

For the first time in her life, Alex did not want to go to school the next day. Like a robot she dressed, ate, brushed her teeth and was off. By the time second break came around she was on the verge of internally collapsing as she calmly walked down the corridor a neutral expression on her face as she passed other students.

She was ushered into the room, unaccompanied this time, and sat on the same spot on the floor. As promised, she was handed a book. Unconsciously hugging the book she sat silent listening to Ms Carmichael talk. Occasionally there was a question that she had to answer, but mainly she was silent, setting the pattern for the next few weeks. One of the other students seeing Ms Carmichael for a similar problem met up with Alex and started a conversation which ended up in an explanation of how to correctly slit your wrists to commit suicide. She wasn't suicidal, but Alex filed that information away for later use. Finally Ms Carmichael uttered the words that Alex had been dreading. "We need to tell your parents."

Despite Alex's begging and pleading, her parents were called in and Ms Carmichael explained the situation to them. Alex didn't dare look her parents in the eyes. She focused on the deck of cards in her hands, continuously shuffling them. Alex listened as Ms Carmichael explained that this was not a cry for attention but something very serious that needed to be treated before it became worse. She emphasised that it was nobody's fault and that Alex had probably been suffering from depression for years. Alex mentally shook her head. She did not have depression. Sure, she hurt herself on purpose, but that had nothing to do with anything. It was just a way to explain the pain to herself, a way to release the build up of emotions that constricted her throat and held her heart in their talons. She would never be able to explain that to her parents, and now they would leave the meeting believing that she had depression and should be on medication and should see psychiatrists and psychologists and all that nonsense that she didn't need.

The car ride home was quiet. Each person was locked in their own thought bubble trying to process the information from the meeting. Grant began to moan that he had found the way Alex kept shuffling the cards extremely disrespectful and that she shouldn't have done that. She should have been a part of the meeting. Karen asked her if she was going to do it again and Alex said no. Karen just nodded.

After supper that night before bed Alex drew the knife across her shoulder several times. The pain inside was unbearable and she needed to release it. If she was careful and only cut places people could not see then there would be no problem. Nobody would know and life could carry on as it should. Her parents could forget the whole thing happened and she would no longer be a failure to them. She would no longer be the worst example of a big sister that anyone could ever have.

If they did not know about the cuts, they could not stop loving her because they existed.

For the rest of the year she continued meeting with Ms Carmichael once a week. They never got down to the root of Alex's problem. Ms Carmichael assumed Alex was seeing a Psychologist as had been recommended at the meeting, and Alex had the sneaky suspicion that the councillor knew Alex was lying when she said that the cutting had stopped.

She told the same thing to her parents, she even showed them her feet and legs as proof. They never queried the fact that her shoulders were never bared, even when swimming. So the Rivers assumed that Alex was getting counselling at school and Ms Carmichael assumed that Alex was getting help externally. It was a tough job convincing both parties and making sure that they did not suspect anything. She had so many masks and lies up in the air that she was trying to juggle and control that at times she felt completely drained. Once or twice she wondered what would happen if she just let the balls drop and let the truth come out, but she never dared.

Then Melissa found out and added her voice in support. After a particularly tiring conversation Alex gave Melissa permission to tell the pastor of the church what was happening. He recommended a good psychologist and when Alex presented this option to her parents they were extremely upset that she had been cutting all the while. They kept asking why, and she kept saying that she didn't know. How do you explain that you need to release an internal pain that has no reason to exist by making it external, though nothing had happened to cause the pain in the first place?

So Alex diligently went to see the psychologist, who would ask questions that Alex would find ways to answer in the most innocent ways possible so as to give away the least amount of information about herself. After the psychologist locked her in another room so that she could speak with Alex's parents about her brother Peter, who was having problems with Social Phobia, Alex refused to go back. She had put up with the questions, she had put up with being spoken to like a child or someone of lesser intelligence, but she would not put up with being locked out of her own psychology session so that they could discuss her brother.

Alex assured her parents that she had stopped cutting and the issue faded into the background as Peter's issues became the focus. Trying to get him to school when he physically couldn't move, taking him to a psychiatrist, making sure he took his Ritalin.

Ms Carmichael promised that she would see Alex through to Matric, her final year of school, and even though she was still cutting as the year ended there was the potential that the following year something could be done.

Two months into the next year Ms Carmichael left the school for a post elsewhere. The cutting became worse and more frequent but Alex hid it very well. The physical pain of her uniform rubbing over the scabs on her shoulders every day reminded her that she deserved the pain. Reminded her that she could still feel the pain.

And the darkness laughed in her face when she tried to convince herself that she could control the cutting – she could stop if she wanted to. No help needed.

Grant and Karen remained oblivious to the fact that scar after scar was being added to their daughter's body. And so grade ten and grade eleven passed as if nothing sinister was happening. They flew by on a snail's wings marked only by significant events like birthdays or the first time Alex tried to take an overdose. She never told her parents about the overdose attempt, because she had failed, again, at something else. She just pretended she had a stomach bug and went on with life as if she was normal.

T he final year of high school started like the years before. Timetables, lessons, teachers, assemblies, darkness and cutting.

That year Peter and Adrian began grade eight at the same high school as Alex. She watched as Adrian excelled in academics and Peter made the top sports sides for his age group. Alex still cut, and still nobody knew, but mainly she wrote. The cutting was only for emergencies when words could not contain the pain.

Full of hate and loathing Alex flirted with Anorexia and Bulimia, finding the former to work better. Even though she could make herself gag nothing would come up, so she started skipping meals when she could get away with her parents not noticing, gave her school sandwiches to hungry classmates and refused food when offered at other's houses unless she absolutely had to accept. She never lost any weight, neither did she gain, but she felt in control. She could decide when to eat. If she didn't want to, no matter how loudly her stomach complained, she didn't have to. She just wished that she would lose even the smallest amount, just enough that she could look beautiful, like all the other girls. When she failed to control her food, and ate something she thought she shouldn't, there was a mental switch and she would binge, eating whatever was in sight until she was so full she could not bring herself to even look at a glass of water. The guilt that followed that food into her stomach always made her try turn to Bulimia, which never worked, and so she would eventually return to not eating at all.

Her parents did not notice this particular pattern, because they were having trouble with Peter. He could not bring himself to go to school. He would get dressed in his uniform, have breakfast, pack his bag, and sit on the edge of the bed. But when it came to standing up and walking out of the door he simply couldn't do it. He could not force his calves to push him to his feet or ankles to move him from the room. At first they tried adjusting his Ritalin dose in hopes that that would work, but it didn't. Then the Rivers resorted to a psychiatrist who diagnosed Peter with a Social Phobia – his brain was simply overwhelmed by the people.

Every morning there was a battle as Karen and Grant tried various ways to persuade Peter to stand up and leave the house. Alex and Adrian were encouraged to encourage him, to try to motivate him, but the situation was embarrassing to him and they could see that. Peter was a strong boy who excelled at cricket and hockey. He was a man, not a wimp, and to have to be coddled like a baby with platitudes and cuddles to try and entice him to get up for school was embarrassing and hurtful. They meant well, but Karen and Grant did not see that involving his siblings was only embarrassing him more. Adrian and Alex noticed, knew what he was feeling, so they blatantly ignored their parent's instructions and treated Peter as if he was going to go to school the same as them. They made no fuss, paid him no special attention, and took the verbal lashings from their parents for not trying to help their brother. Some days were good days and Peter went to school, but eventually the mountains of work he had missed began to loom over him, causing him extra anxiety. He was not stupid, he was very intelligent and especially good with maths. Still the pressure to catch up the work he had missed, not being able to pass the tests or eventually the grade itself fed his social phobia, just as her intentional isolation fed Alex's darkness.

To a greater extent than Peter knew at the time Alex could identify with his problems. Every morning she would watch the coaxing end in shouting and a hurried dash to the car with Grant fuming the entire journey because Peter wasn't doing what he was told, and her heart would ache for her brother. If she could have taken his social phobia onto her own shoulders she would gladly have born that burden for him. He deserved to show his intelligence and get an education to allow him the best possible future. Peter missed out on most of the second and third term, and when he

94

was at school some of his classmates would tease him about being away for so long and so often. This bullying and teasing just chased him back to bed and into his shell.

Alex figured out a pattern where she could skip breakfast and lunch and just eat supper without anyone knowing, and even though she never lost weight she wasn't gaining any. That factor being in suspension helped her feel slightly better about herself. Yes, she was fat and ugly, but she wasn't getting fatter and uglier. Still she watched the willowy popular girls with their boyfriends who would hold their hands and caress their cheeks and longed for someone to see that inside of her was a willowy girl longing to be loved by someone, someone who could see past the layers of fat and ugliness, past the hurt, maybe even past the darkness.

Being the final year of school, there were several special events. One of these was the Matric Dance.

Most girls started planning their outfits in January even though the dance was in July. Alex didn't even want to begin planning anything. There was no dress in the world that would make her look like a princess. She would merely look like an elephant in a tent. She began skipping as many suppers as she could in the vague hope that maybe she would lose just some weight by July so that she could have a pretty dress and show that despite being ugly there was pretty within her.

It didn't work, out of desperation she decided to go with an African print skirt and top – because a ball gown would have looked like a marquis. She decided that she would have her hair braided in the traditional African style, and spent three painful hours the Saturday before the dance sitting dead still in a chair while a colleague of her mom's pulled and twisted and plaited until her hair was full of braids. That night was her grandparents wedding anniversary and they went to a fancy restaurant to celebrate. One look at her and her aunts and uncles turned away and started other conversations. Her cousins ignored her and spoke with her siblings and Alex sat at the table playing with the cutlery. Her aunt and uncle were visiting from Australia with her youngest cousin and her grandparents were so proud to have their youngest son in the country with them to celebrate this occasion.

The food was delicious, but she tasted nothing. She felt like an ugly duckling, a rotten apple, something that didn't belong. She ate mechanically, and ordered as much alcohol as her parents would allow her to drink, but nothing numbed the mental pain that was consuming her. That night at home she tried to write it out. The page stared back at her mocking her with its blankness as the pen trembled, touching the paper with a stutter that could not be turned into a sentence. Only her blade could help.

Monday came around – the dance would be on that Saturday coming. She did not have a boyfriend to go with, but a friend of hers who had been in the same band as her but had matriculated the year before had agreed to go with her. Dressed in uniform, hair in braids, Alex set out for school that Monday morning.

Half-way through the day there was a general knowledge event. Alex had decided to be brave and take part, so she was a member of one of the teams seated in the hall during break while those not interested fooled about outside. She didn't exactly have fun, but it wasn't an entirely bad experience. Some of her answers were right, to the surprise of her group, and most of those answers came from the fact that she read whenever she could. After the event it was break time and she was making her way down the corridor when the teacher in charge of the Matrics called her name. Alex turned.

"Alex, Mr Fisher says that you cannot be seen in school uniform with your hair like that." Alex blinked. What was wrong with her hair? She had been born in Africa – she was African. Sure, she was a white African, but the black Africans braided their hair all the time and even managed to somehow sneak different colours in without a reprimand. "Go home." He commanded

Tears of injustice clogging her throat Alex phoned home and explained to her mother why she had to be fetched. Her mother agreed that it was unfair and the family spoke about it that evening. It was agreed that they would wait to raise the issue as there was a meeting the following day involving Peter and his poor attendance record.

Alex dressed in casual clothes, civvies, and went to school the next day. If you missed school during the week leading up to the dance you were not allowed to attend the dance. Many people asked her why she was in civvies and she told them about the previous day's conversation. Most brushed it off, some took offence. Again roughly half-way through the day she was called out of class to the teacher in charge of her year. "Alex, you can't be at school with your hair like that."

"Sir, yesterday you said I couldn't be seen in my uniform with my hair in braids. I am not in my uniform, I am in civvies. I am following the rule you gave me yesterday." There was a brief pause that made Alex think that perhaps the teacher agreed with what she was saying. However the principal had given him a message and he had to deliver it.

"Alex, you cannot be seen at school with your hair like that. White people cannot wear braids." He winced at the words. "Phone your mother, go home."

Again Alex was fetched from school and that evening her mother spent hours rubbing conditioner into her hair to loosen the braids and remove them from her head. Alex sat mute at her desk as braid after braid landed in the bin. It had cost money to have her hair done, money they could not afford, and now it was all a waste. Karen spoke gently with her daughter while she was removing the braids.

"Mr Fisher told Peter that either he comes to school tomorrow or there will be repercussions, so maybe tomorrow he will go." Alex doubted this. "And I know this is not fair on you, but we need to focus on what is happening with Peter right now. We don't want to raise any more trouble with Mr Fisher when he is already fed up with Peter." Alex winced as something pulled. "And yes both your father and I know that it is racist what he said and how he has treated you, but there is nothing we can do at this point except what he has asked." Finally the last braid was thrown away and Alex went to wash her hair.

She struggled to sleep that night, and lying in bed she kept hearing Peter walking to and from the bathroom. Something niggled in her mind that this was not right. He should not be going to the bathroom so many times – something was wrong. However she brushed off that niggle and turned over to fall into a restless pit of tormenting dreams. Instead of her alarm waking her the next morning it was the shrill cry of her mother. "Grant! Come quickly! Peter's taken something!"

Both Lauren and Alex jumped out of bed and reached the room Peter and Adrian shared before their father had even registered that he had been called. There was Peter, lying on the bed. Limp, lifeless, barely breathing surrounded by all the medication he had been able to get his hands on during the night. Grant lifted his son's arm and let it go. It flopped upon his face with enough force to bruise his nose – Peter didn't move. Adrian helped their father get Peter into the car and they rushed him to Oakwood General. Lauren went to school, but Alex refused to leave her mother's side. She kept hearing Peter's footsteps as he trudged to and from the bathroom the night before. She kept remembering that niggle that had tried to tell her to get out of bed. And she could not get the picture of his lifeless body lying sprawled across the bed.

If she had gotten up he would not be on his way to the emergency unit. If he died the blame would lie squarely, and heavily, upon her shoulders. The darkness laughed at her weakness, taunting her and mocking her, making her believe that she had made the decision to sleep when she knew something was wrong and if her brother did not wake up it would be her fault.

Alex made her mother a cup of coffee and waited for her uncle to arrive to take them to the hospital. All she could do was look after her mother while the darkness branded her with the guilt. She felt she could only try and undo the pain and fear that coursed through her mother as she saw the sight no mother should see, her son motionless on his bed surrounded by empty boxes and bottles.

Too scared to hug her mother, Alex kept herself busy making phone calls to the pastor and the children's pastor, although Peter didn't attend church. Her uncle drove them to the hospital and on the way Karen phoned the head teacher, Mr Fisher. Just to inform him of what was happening.

Alex wanted to grab the phone and yell at him that he was an insensitive asshole who didn't give a damn about his students but just wanted to keep a perfect attendance and academic record. That he was a racist bigot and wouldn't know how to be a decent person even if God himself descended from heaven to show him how. Instead, she seethed inside and resented the idiot principal who had not looked further than the image of the school.

At the hospital Karen went into the emergency room while Alex waited outside. The pastor arrived and briefly hugged Alex before heading into the room to comfort Karen and Grant. She stood in the waiting room, hugging herself as tightly as she could, she didn't know if praying would work. It seemed to her that God loved the members of the church who were really spiritual and even though she was part of the music ministry, singing almost every Sunday, and part of the children's ministry and the Friday night programs for the young children, she was not spiritual enough. The darkness made sure she believed she could never be good enough or spiritual enough. She couldn't believe that God would love her, because nobody else did. And if man was created in God's image, why had he screwed up when creating her? She felt like a practical joke God had pulled on the world. As if he was sitting up in Heaven with the angels laughing as she tripped and stumbled over every obstacle thrown her way.

But she tried praying. Maybe if the prayer was for someone else God would listen? She tried fancy words but the same sentence kept repeating itself over and over in her head:

"God, please don't let me have killed my brother."

After the overdose attempt Peter came home and everything returned to a semblance of normality. Everyone was gentle around him and he soon learned to use that to his advantage to get anything he wanted, even if it could not be afforded. Alex watched him manipulate their parents and watched her parents give him everything he wanted out of fear of losing him.

Studying for her final exams Alex found the atmosphere in the house too tense and electric so Melissa offered up her house as a place to study. Grant would often drop her at Melissa's where, from time to time, Melissa's parents would look in on her and bring her tea. Mostly they left her alone and forgot she was there and every now and then the family dog would wander into the room and sniff her leg as if to make sure that she was ok before trotting out again. Alex felt comfortable enough about the arrangement that she managed to get her study done in time for the exams to start.

Her anxious mother arrived with Peter in the car to collect her after one particularly nasty Afrikaans exam. As Peter was seeing double and could barely walk they had to take him straight to the emergency unit. While he lay on a bed in the hospital and their mother tried to phone his unavailable psychiatrist, Alex sat beside him and sang to him. She sang every song that came into her head, whether she remembered all the lyrics or not. When the doctors could find nothing medically wrong with him they sent him home as if nothing was wrong.

Later that night Alex found Peter digging in her cupboard. Asking him what he was doing, he responded that he was looking for paper so she thought nothing more of it. Something bothered her at the back of her mind though, something she knew should be remembering.

The memory didn't connect to the front of her mind until Lauren remarked to their parents that Peter was walking to and from the bathroom with glasses of water. She realised that she had paracetamol in her cupboard as well as paper. How could she have been so stupid! Why would he have wanted paper? He wasn't a writer the way she was so he wouldn't need it. He must have been taking the tablets she'd had in there.

Their father held her brother to the bed and forced out as many tablets as he could get from his son, then rushed him back to the hospital. Peter was so weak that he couldn't get into the car, he fell into her arms and she helped him up and lay with his head in her lap while she stroked his hair throughout the speedy trip. The brother she knew would never show weakness like this, he would never let his head be stroked, would certainly never lie with his head in his sister's lap.

The hospital staff could see the state he was in but simply fed him charcoal and sent him home. Alex was infuriated, wondering how they could care so little. He was a human, not just some stray animal, he was suffering and they were sending him home just because he wasn't medically ill.

All the while the darkness inside laughed and jeered, taunting her that she had failed. She was supposed to be the big sister, the one who looked after the younger three. She was a failure; she had permitted him another attempt she believed she could have prevented. Her brother had nearly died twice and both times she should have prevented him getting at the medications.

When he tried again that night by taking all of Karen's diabetes tablets so his sugar dipped dangerously low they finally had to take him to a state facility that had a ward for psychiatric patients. When the charcoal had taken affect and his sugar levels had stabilised, they transferred him to the C23 ward, where they put all the crazies. He was there for a few days but the care was terrible so, on the advice of a psychiatrist, he was transferred to a private clinic.

Every day he would jump the wall and run away from the clinic. Each day Karen received a phone call from the fast-food shop nearest the clinic and it would always be Peter begging to be collected. The next day they would take him back and the process would start again. They only managed to get him to stay in the building once and as a reward they let him come home for the weekend. Alex knew he wouldn't go back on the Monday, but everyone assured her that he would and she had nothing to worry about. She stayed awake the whole weekend watching the passage for any signs of Peter leaving his room. She would not fail again. She would not let her brother die.

Monday came and he refused to go back to the clinic. The head of the unit came to try persuading him back but Peter simply ignored him.
"Would he stay if I went with him?" Alex eventually demanded, unable to bear the thought of her brother being forced to go somewhere he didn't like. Both her mother and the unit head looked at her. Then the head

of the unit nodded slowly. Alex silently left them there as she went to pack. She was gathering her toiletries when her mother followed her into the room.

"You're still cutting aren't you?" Karen asked

"Yes." Was the only reply her daughter could make.

Karen nodded but could think of nothing else to say so she helped her daughter pack the things she would need for her stay at the clinic.

The clinic was the most pointless thing Alex had ever done. Yes, it kept Peter there and stopped him from running away, but she learned nothing from any of the 'sessions' except that counsellors were exceptionally easy to con and manipulate even while they were bragging about being able to recognise manipulative behaviour. Peter would be as good as a trained dog during the week, following the program and doing what was expected of him. Every Friday he would set his weekend goals, and then every weekend at home he would be the same person he was before he entered the clinic. Come Monday's he would eloquently explain how he had completed his goals and how good he had been over the weekend. Put simply, he bullshit his way through six weeks of sessions which taught him nothing of use. Alex learnt nothing of benefit either, except that it was very easy to deceive people. By the end of her stay in the clinic Alex was completely disillusioned, the place was supposed to be a professional institution, with doctors that knew how to help, yet they had not helped at all. It seemed to her that she must have been beyond help, just too dark for any light to get through.

Life went back to normal. Soon the family began to treat Peter more like a human and less like a delicate figurine. Alex got her final results and passed all her subjects, just scraping through in mathematics. She applied to study teaching and was accepted into the university. Eagerly, yet with trepidation, she waited for the new educational year to begin so her tertiary education could start. Maybe she would finally make something of herself. Maybe she would finally make friends, be part of a group that wanted her around, maybe she could fit in…

The darkness cackled silently. University was just another opportunity to prove its strength and its ability to completely immobilise her. It relished the thought of new people to chase away, new chances to prove its dominance, new ways to make her its own.

Her mind began filling with doubts. What if she couldn't do the coursework? What if there were group projects and nobody wanted to be in her group? What if she was so pathetic, so ugly that it chased people away before they had a chance to speak with her? Would they even let her voice her opinions or would she be forced to become yet another sheep in another setting?

Fear strangled her, gripped her throat and made it hard for her to breathe, her blade became a constant friend and her shoulders ached daily. The dried scabs from her cuts, rubbing off under clothing that scratched and itched. It was not the same feeling she had when she cut and the blood escaped in a great whoosh as she let out the breath she had been holding for too long. She felt every time she moved as an irritation of pain, she felt alive, reminding her that she deserved all pain because of what she was and who she was.

Few people knew about the continued cutting, her parents thought that the clinic had cured their daughter. Only Beth and Melissa knew. Beth knew because she bluntly asked and received an equally blunt answer. Melissa knew because Alex would speak to her through the poems she gave her every week.

The darkness within was part of her, it was her, so she knew nothing could cure her of it. She bore the blame for Peter's near-death solely on her own. She lived with the fact that she was worthless that she was a failure who should have never existed. Her eating became more erratic and she often went days without anything to eat or to drink on purpose. Each time she let the blade bite into her shoulder she proved to herself that she was still alive. Each time she punched a wall and opened up wounds upon her knuckles the pain brought her peace, because she deserved it. Each time she swallowed bleach to try and make herself sick she hoped that it would be the last time she would have to try.

Why was God punishing her? Why was she being kept alive? Was it just for his amusement, so he could throw obstacles into her path and watch her struggle?

Throughout the darkness and danger she was certain of one truth - she deserved the pain.

A new year and a new chance at figuring out how to beat this darkness rolled around. Some days were not so bad. She didn't exactly see the sun but the clouds weren't as black. Most days she wandered around in a haze of pain and jumbled up emotions that came up from nowhere at unexpected times to trip her up and scare her into silence. She never spoke about the darkness. She didn't understand it herself, and how could she explain something that she didn't understand? All she knew was that it was in her and that it spoke the truth about her. It broadcast every flaw, every tiny imperfection unavoidably and deafeningly into the very core of her being.

University was much like school. Cliques that Alex was not part of quickly grew up, group projects where she was not welcome and her input was not considered were assigned. Snickers and giggles behind her back were barely concealed. She went back to her old habit of carrying a book with her wherever she went and would often arrive early to a class and sit reading, trying to absorb as much peace as possible before the lecture began.

Classes weren't hard, but they weren't easy. She loved English however. It had long since been her favourite subject, and the lecturer she had that year was passionate about what he was teaching to the point of sometimes leaving the slower members of the class behind. He once caught her writing down a quick poem before he started lecturing, the idea had popped into her head and she had wanted to write it before it got lost, and was very surprised at the talent that was right under his nose. Alex took his compliments with more than a pinch of salt. It was just a poem and she though it wasn't a particularly good one even.

January became February then March. Her darkness consumed her and most of her poetry was filled with the thoughts and feelings that it brought to the surface. The only person who knew those feelings was Melissa.

Then that Sunday arrived. A day that burned in her memory for the rest of her life.

Alex was on the roster to sing that morning and Melissa was the team leader. Before each morning service, while the early service was happening, the music team would meet in the prayer room and pray. That Sunday, after the praying was done and everyone was collecting their instruments and moving from the room, Alex handed Melissa an envelope containing several poems. One of the poems bore the title "Only in my Head" in which she explained that all these feelings were just things in her head and perhaps not actually real truths. Melissa took the envelope and looked at it.
"I don't want to read any more of your poems. You are too negative." She said as she handed back the envelope.

Blood rushed to Alex's ears and she could have sworn someone was beating on her eardrums. Her friend, the one person she had trusted enough to talk through her poems to about the darkness, the only one she's shared the part of her that nobody else knew about with, had just told her that she did not want to hear any more. Alex somehow managed to look Melissa in the eyes, and all the kindness and caring that usually filled them was full of hatred, loathing and disgust.

Nodding, Alex stepped back and then walked from the room to the kitchen around the corner. She took each poem out of the envelope and shredded them one by one into the bin at her feet. Each tear was like tearing her heart, because those words were her heart. They were her soul – her core. They were the real her that didn't hide behind the mask because she didn't have to. As the last piece of envelope fluttered into the bin Alex took a deep breath and arranged her face into perfect neutrality. Then she walked out of the kitchen and over to the rest of the group, joining in the light banter as though nothing had happened.

During the set time for the music team to play, there was a customary break in the music where the leader normally said a prayer or read a scripture to encourage the members of the congregation.

Melissa started talking, but she did not pick up her Bible or close her eyes in prayer. She just spoke from her heart.

"We are a family – the body of Christ. Each one of us plays a vital role in the workings of the church. Think of the human body. If one part is not working the whole body can begin to shut down and eventually there could be death. We need to support each other. Help carry each other's burdens."

She took a breath. "We need to be open and honest with each other, sharing what is on our hearts no matter how negative it is."

Alex felt her spine stiffen. She felt as if she had just been slapped in the face. How could this woman sit there behind the piano and say that, when not even twenty minutes ago she had told Alex that she was too negative. Alex didn't know if she wanted to shout and scream or curl up and cry, but in that moment one thing was perfectly clear. Apparently in the church there were rules, one set for the congregation, and one set for her. Two standards set, one for everyone and another to be applied only to Alex. The standards set for her were so high that she could never hope to reach them. She understood that she would never be good enough, never be spiritual enough. Numbly she sang the final few songs and the service continued. She did not hear another word preached that morning. All that swirled around her brain were the words 'too negative', like a horrific chant in a vicious cyclone of darkness. All that filled her heart was the pain she'd felt at the look of disgust in Melissa's eyes earlier that morning.

That afternoon Alex attempted another overdose. She never had any idea what she took; she just took whatever she could find. She woke up slightly nauseous but still went to the evening service. That night she cut with twice the ferocity and deeper than she had cut before as though in an attempt to dig the pain from her soul.

After that Alex didn't speak. She simply sat in silence and watched. There were other people who had darkness like she did, and Melissa welcomed them with open arms. Alex didn't feel jealous, she felt afraid. What if Melissa abandoned them like she had abandoned Alex? She wanted to go over to them and tell them to be careful. She wanted to tell them to watch their backs, to put something in place to help prop them up in case they were left alone and lost the way she had been.

When she had to be near Melissa Alex simply plastered on her mask as thick as she could manage and answered all questions giving away little if any information. She made herself appear normal, appear the way she thought she should have been created.

Later that year, a family joined the church, coming all the way from Canada because of a job opening. Matthew, Helen and their young son Sam. Helen got up during a time in the service where the congregation was encouraged to share a verse or something that was in their heart.

She read from the Bible about the prophets of Baal verses Elijah in the battle of the ultimate God. She read about how the prophets of Baal prayed to their God, whipping and harming themselves in order to please him. Then she closed the Bible.

"I used to harm myself." She confessed into the total silence the congregation awarded her.

Beneath the silence was a layer of acceptance, Alex sat in the gallery shaking slightly. She was amazed at what courage Helen had to be able to admit that… and once again appalled at the apparent separate rule for herself. She felt that if she had admitted that she hurt herself she would have been drummed out of the church on the spot.

"I haven't done it for ten years now, but I used to. I just want to tell you that you don't need to do that to make God listen to you. He listens to the whispers of your heart. You don't have to hurt yourself, for any reason." Helen continued before she sat down again and the service continued.

After the service Alex gathered all the courage she could, which wasn't enough to even fill a thimble, and walked over to Helen. Hand shaking, she raised it slightly and tapped Helen's shoulder. The short woman with the shoulder-length black hair turned and looked directly into Alex's eyes – her dark eyes neutral yet calming at the same time.

"Can...may...I..." Alex swallowed the desert that had taken root in her throat as Helen waited patiently. "Can I talk to you?"

Helen nodded and the two of them made their way to the closest pew. Haltingly and with many pauses to gather herself, Alex spoke.

"What you said, about the cutting, about you, that was brave. I...I cut myself." For the first time Alex said the words out loud. "I would appreciate....well could you.....maybe, if you wanted to or had the time..." Alex stumbled over her words but Helen waited patiently as if there was all the time in the world. "Would you pray for me?"

"Is there anything specific you want me to pray for?" Helen asked.

Alex thought for a moment. She was unsure how much information could she give Helen – how much of the darkness could she share without chasing her away the way she had with Melissa.

"No, nothing in particular." Alex finally managed to mumble. Although Helen raised a brow as if she knew Alex wasn't telling the whole truth, she prayed anyway.

"Thank you." Alex managed to make her gratefulness known though she still felt as though her throat was closed for the rest of time.

"My pleasure." Helen smiled. "Any time you need to talk I'm here, and so is Matthew."

Alex stood as her phone rang and her father announced that he had arrived to fetch her. As she walked out the building she looked back at the short, sturdy woman sitting on the pew. Their eyes met and something tiny sparked inside Alex. She wondered if just maybe, possibly she had just met the person she really needed – a true friend.

oth Helen and Matthew were qualified sound engineers, something which Oakwood Baptist sorely needed to improve the quality of sound when their music teams played. Matthew began teaching the current team how to actually work the equipment as well as playing bass during many services, as he was an extremely accomplished bassist.

As Alex's friendship with the Swan's grew Matthew began teaching her small tips and tricks about playing bass. It wasn't long before Alex was playing bass for almost every service, much to the delight of the congregation who seemed to enjoy her playing and singing. The other bassists weren't reliable and never turned up for practice or on the day they were supposed to play –For the first time in her life Alex felt that maybe she had a place where she could belong. She felt she was good with picking up rhythms, melodies and memorising lyrics, soon she was singing and playing at the same time – much to the delight of the music team leaders who were also running out of singers.

Alex missed out on second year of university due to a torn ankle ligament that set her back a semester. Grant was able to get the year's fees waved, because it was due to negligence on behalf of the university that she had slipped and fallen, and the following year she started with second year. Scholastically things were going great. She enjoyed the projects and assignments and was beginning to accept that she would never be as smart as the other students. Unfortunately internally, things were not so good at all.

In her quiet supportive way, Helen had somehow persuaded Alex to give psychologists one more try. She had never actually uttered the words 'go see a psychologist', but by telling Alex snippets of her life story she managed to impart the idea that outside, professional help was needed. One of the church members had recently graduated with a degree in psychology and was now the church's official clinical pastoral therapist. One particularly emotional service left Alex shaken, trying to recover her mask before she left the building.

"Why don't you go and talk to Jen?" Helen suggested, her concern showing.

Alex thought about it. Jen knew her family through school connections so Alex wondered if she would tell her parents what was said? Watching Jen talk with someone down at the front of the church who was in tears, Alex saw her gentle manner and the calming effect she had on the person. Her chicken of courage had been plucked so many times it barely had any feathers, but she plucked what she could and walked over to Jen. Tapping her on the shoulder Alex got her attention.

"I need to talk to you." She tried nervously.

Jen indicated the seat beside her and haltingly Alex tried to explain the darkness. All she could explain was the fact that she hurt herself, and then no words would come out. Her mouth opened and closed like a goldfish and eventually she just shut it and slumped forward. "Never mind, it's ok." Alex stood up. "We can't afford it. I'm fine." She began to walk away and Jen gently grabbed her arm.

"I will arrange something."

So Alex began seeing Jen weekly. The first few sessions were spent in almost absolute silence while Alex tried to figure out if she could trust this person or not. Eventually Jen figured out that Alex responded better when asked questions instead of just blurting out her feelings, and soon therapy was happening. Jen recommended that Alex see a psychiatrist for her depression so she could get medical help, but Alex refused. She was not depressed. She had not been depressed when she was eleven, nor when she was thirteen, nor fourteen, and certainly not now when she was twenty. She just needed help because she was hurting herself that was all.

It had been four months since Alex had last picked up the knife, and each day was becoming harder than the next. It called to her from its hiding place and she often found herself daydreaming about what it would feel like to have it bite into her skin once again. She held on though. She did not know what she was holding on to, but she held on.

Then in an attempt to regulate her erratic and sometimes nonexistent eating patterns Alex had joined Weight Watchers. It had only been a week, but she had stuck to the program faithfully – only to have picked up weight at the end of the week. This crushed her hopes, again, and brought back to stark reality the fact that she was an utter failure at everything she tried her hand at. She couldn't see through the darkness to the fact that she was a good bass player, that she was a good singer and a vital part of the music team. That she wrote exceptionally well, that her level of communication, when she chose to speak, was always excellent. That she read so well aloud that the older ladies of the church always enjoyed when she read because they could hear every word no matter how deaf they were. The darkness hid those things. All she saw in her head were the bright red numbers from the scale showing her failure, and all she heard was the darkness reminding her over and over that whatever she did, she failed at so why even try.

That night Alex took her knife and went to sit in the garden. She rested the blade on her leg and looked at it glowing in the light of the street lamp behind her. It seemed to have a Heavenly glow – like one sees around the halos of angels in pictures. She looked up at a random patch of sky and just started talking.

"God, why? Why have you created me? It says that everyone was created for a purpose, but what purpose could I possibly fulfil? I'm a failure, I'm weak and pathetic. I hate how I have been created and wish with all my power that you hadn't created me. How can you possibly use me? Melissa once said that you could use my writing as a way to help others, but how can I believe her now? After what she did to me? Was she just lying to make me feel better? You have gifted the other church members with so many talents, why not me?"

She began to twirl the knife between her fingers as tears she'd held back for aeons burst through the self-imposed dam of will power and pride to saturate her face.

"God, why am I alive? Am I just your idea of a practical joke? How can you love me when I am just so bad inside? When I am dark and nobody likes me at all? – How can you love me when nobody else does? And the things I do, they don't honour you at all. I am a terrible example of a Christian; I am not spiritual enough to be a part of your church. Why? Oh, God, why?"

The only answer was the silence of the night and a slight edge to a breeze that had appeared suddenly. Shaking her head and spraying tears around her Alex picked up the knife and kissed it. Then she slid it into her skin – at her wrist, where her watch strap would be able to hide the mark. Except this time she pressed too hard and the cut was gaping like an eye. Blood trickled over her hand and stained the grass beneath her as she began to panic. She knew she wasn't dying, but she would have to explain this to her parents because this wound needed stitches. Not knowing what to do Alex sent an emergency text to a new friend who she had recently become close to.

Susan was there within ten minutes and gently took the knife from Alex before examining the wound. With Alex's permission she called in two more friends, one of whom was studying medicine. All three agreed that the wound needed stitches. Susan accompanied Alex inside where she stood in the lounge with her parents looking at her.

"I…I need to go to the hospital." Alex mumbled into the floor.

"Why?" Karen asked with an edge in her voice that made Alex suspect that her mother already knew the answer to that question.

Mutely Alex removed her watch and showed her wrist with its open wound. Her mother started crying and her father started shouting while she just stood there in shame.

Susan accompanied Alex to the hospital and stood at her bedside while the doctor stitched her wrist. Throughout the procedure the doctor lectured on how suicide was pathetic and a coward's way out. How it upset the family of the person and the friends and how it was a selfish act on behalf of the deceased. Karen began to tense and Alex switched off and focussed on the curtains in front of her. After the doctor was gone and the nurse was doing the final cleaning and bandaging, she apologised for the doctor. But Karen was already of the opinion that medical personnel were uncaring and did not understand how complex something like this was.

Alex had an emergency session with Jen the next day, and after a lot of persuasion finally admitted that maybe, just maybe, she was slightly depressed and needed medical help. Jen didn't push it further than that, because she knew that the defeat in Alex's voice at admitting that fact was genuine. Alex did not want to be labelled as a crazy person. She did not want to have medication she would have to take forever, or have to try explaining to people why she was upset when nothing had happened.

Her first psychiatrist tried a few different medications on Alex, but before they could perfect the drug or the dosage she left the country for Germany. Alex went back to the way she was without medication. She continued to see Jen once a week and Jen tried to get her to see the psychiatrist who had replaced the one that had left, but Alex was against it completely.

Then one day in the shower she sliced her shoulder deep enough to need another hospital trip and stitches. It was a different doctor stitching the wound this time, but even though there was no lecture there was an air of anger at having to stitch up a self-made wound. After that, objection or not, Alex was sent to the psychiatrist. Dr Glass.

More medical experimentations took place and in between were more overdose attempts nobody knew about. Two of those attempts were paracetamol and Alex had no idea, nor did she care, about the damage she was doing to her liver. Finally one of the medications seemed to help. The feelings of failure, hopelessness, emptiness, worthlessness and pain were held back and Alex simply felt numb. She did not stop cutting though. By now it was more than a way to release the emotions bottled up inside of her, by now part of it was an addiction.

Yes, she used the cutting to help her body release all the pain and emotions that built up inside of her, but sometimes she found herself picking up the blade and slicing herself just because she wanted to cut and see the blood. The line between a coping method and an addiction was blurring and she found herself sometimes cutting for the sake of seeing the blood and not as a release from the pain. It always released the pain inside, but sometimes she knew that the pain was not bad enough to need releasing.

Alex did not thrive on the medication, but it offered a small pedestal for her mind to stand on within the darkness so that it did not drown completely.

At the age of twenty Alex had to admit what Mrs Edwards had noticed nine years previously, and what her pre-school teachers had failed to notice: She suffered from depression.

Opening the front door to see who had rung the doorbell one day, Alex was momentarily stunned at the handsome man in front of her. He introduced himself as Frans and said that he was there to LAN with Peter. Alex let him in and left the two of them to their game. Later that night she created a World of Warcraft account to see what it was like and soon the game was one of her favourites.

She and Frans would chat using mIRC or MSN and soon he knew much more about her than she knew about him. She finally decided that she had liked him from afar for way too long, and asked him out. His condition was that she stop cutting, and so she did. There was no anniversary, nothing special to celebrate, one day they were friends and the next they were seeing each other. So Alex picked a day for them to share though Frans didn't seem to care.

The next year brought with it more psychiatric complications. Outside her house one Sunday, Helen had offered to give Alex lifts home from church to save the Rivers petrol money that they could not afford, Alex found her hands and arms frozen. It was as if she was paralyzed. She could not curl a finger, shrug her shoulders or even twitch her muscles. She started shaking out of panic and Helen escorted her inside and explained to the Rivers what had happened – which was nothing.

On a bed in the emergency room later that night, the doctor on duty brushed it off as merely a catatonic state, and had all the nurses come and observe Alex as she could not move her arms nor reposition them to a more comfortable position. She was sent home because there was nothing medically wrong.

The following day sitting in her mother's car outside university, Alex could not move her legs or her arms. She felt paralysed, yet her brain knew that she wasn't.

The darkness laughed at her struggle – pathetic person, couldn't even move when she was supposed to. Just another thing wrong with her...why bother living?

Her psychiatrist tested for neurological reasons, even though he suspected Conversion Disorder, and when there was no neurological cause he confirmed his diagnoses. Alex simply had to ride it out until it left. Sometimes she remained frozen for weeks, sometimes only for a few hours. Each time it happened she knew she was disappointing her parents and causing extra stress upon them. Alex was supposed to be in her third year out of the four she needed to complete her degree, but she hardly made it to university that year as the attacks increased.

Every time she would mention that she was not able to move her father would raise his eyebrows as if he didn't believe her, and her mother would simply sigh. Her brothers became professionals at hoisting her out of the chair and onto the toilet, and her mother forced her to lie on her back to stop her falling out of bed.

Despite the frequency of the paralysing attacks, Alex and Frans went to a braai at Helen and Matthew's house. It was not for any special occasion, just a gathering of friends. Frans was silent to the point of seeming disgusted with her friends and Alex found herself watching him in fear. He was withdrawing from her, she knew it and could feel it, and his attitude towards her friends showed her that he really wasn't interested in anything that had to do with her.

That night Alex took a deep breath and shed her values and morals as her cloths hit the floor. Heart crying stop, her mind forced her onto the bed and let Frans sleep with her. It was not making love. It wasn't even sex in a sense. Alex was not part of the act – her mind was far away and she was crying inside because she had just let her mind rape her heart. Frans was overjoyed and concentrating hard on whatever he was feeling.

Alex watched him, and in the moments his eyes were open she pretended to be part of the act. Eventually it was over and they changed the stained sheets – three drops of innocence that would be washed away.

Frans was still in the mood, but Alex knew that she could not force herself to have him inside her again. So she took him in her mouth and cramped her jaw trying to please him. If she pleased him he would stay. Her hair was pushed to one side and she tried her best to perform an act she had never performed before. Once he exploded she had no clue what to do, so she swallowed and painted on a smile before looking at him. He lay there grinning lopsidedly.
"God, you're good. I'm seeing purple. I don't think I can stand." He smirked

After a while they stood and dressed and each slept on their own side of the bed furthest from the other. Alex did not know what Frans was thinking or dreaming about, but she felt as if she had just been raped…by herself.

The attacks of Conversion Disorder became less frequent, and Alex began spending most weekends at Frans's house. Every weekend the same routine would occur. At nights his parents would go to bed, and Frans would put on a movie – something Science-Fiction or High-Action with lots of noise. Once he was fairly certain that his parents were asleep he would stand and shed his boxers, and Alex would remove her pjammas. She would lie there legs open and trembling, watching the movie with one eye and Frans with the other. She made noises when appropriate, pretended she was on the same page as he was. Her mind was never there. She watched the movies while he thrust in and out of her until he was spent. Then she would smile and say how much she had enjoyed it before sucking him until he was fully spent. Then he would dress, turn out the light and go to bed. Alex would gather her clothes in the dark, get dressed and walk to the spare room where she would try and forget the ache between her legs or the cramps in her locked jaw.

Frans became busy with his studies and Alex became busy with playing bass on Sunday's, so they saw each other less frequently. Soon they were only chatting occasionally over the internet, and Frans would end any conversation Alex tried to initiate with short one-word answers. She had given up everything to keep him, and she was losing him anyway.

Their first year anniversary passed by as if it was an ordinary day. No romantic messages or gifts, in fact they didn't speak with each other that day. Frans had a fear of visiting other people's houses, and because Alex could not get to his place they did not see each other. They never went on a date, never held hands in public because Frans did not like it. He always stood with a gap between them when they stood together and seemed embarrassed to be with her. Small things began to irritate him.

"Why don't you ever wear make-up? It would make you look pretty."

"Walk faster, you're too fat and slow."

"Why did you buy that packet of nuts? It's going to make you fatter."

"Did you wash your hands after stroking the dog?"

"You can't wear that shirt, it has a hole in it. And it's got a design on the front. Change your clothes."

"Why didn't you bother drying your hair before I fetched you? Don't you care about how it makes me look?" He would complain to her whenever the chance arose

Alex tried desperately to hold on to what had been there, but she knew she was failing. The darkness was enjoying every moment, reminding her that nobody could love her or like her because of how she looked, the depression and the failings... no wonder Frans was pulling away.

That March she had a burst ovarian cyst and was away from Church for a week. The next week the roster for the music team came out and Alex's name was not on it. After a meeting with the head of the ministry, where Alex was accompanied by Helen, she was informed that she was off the team because she was 'intimidating' and she 'always sat at the back of the church' and she 'always sat alone' and she 'never attended the prayer meetings'. For every 'reason' that was raised Alex had a valid response – not an excuse, a response. But it had been decided. She was too depressed for the music ministry and so she was kicked off.

A week later the children's pastor called her into a meeting and kicked her off the children's ministry team for the same reason.

She believed she was being told she was not spiritual enough for the church. Her music was taken away from her, the one place she had felt that perhaps God

147

could use her. Working with the children was taken away from her, the one thing she enjoyed the most.

She was too depressed for church. Too depressed to be a Christian, not spiritual enough for anyone at the church. She had to take medication just to get herself to the same level of humanity that came naturally to everybody else. They hated her because of what she was. Everything Melissa had said came back to her – she was just too negative, there was no purpose for her. Bitter tears created salt crystals in her heart and she stopped going to church. She could not look at that stage without her heart aching in a combination of longing to stand on it and hatred towards the people who were on it. She could not sit through a sermon on an amazing God who loved everybody when every cell inside of her cried out that she had never and would never be loved. She could not sit afterwards watching others cry and receive comfort in their pain when she was not allowed to express anything she felt inside.

She remembered a song that they had sung in junior school. "A new commandment I give unto you, that you love one another – as I have loved you. That you love one another – as I have loved you. By this, shall all men know that you are my disciples; if you have love, one for another. By this, shall all men know that you are my disciples; if you have love, one for another."

Alex stopped going to church. The very people who were supposed to be showing her how much God loved her only showed her how much she was despised and hated. They only showed her how much of a freak she was and how unlovable. And she could not bear to enter that building and feel the bitterness grow in her heart at the memory of being kicked out of the only places she felt she was able to have a purpose…because of her darkness; her depression.

No more would she go to church and sit amongst the phoneys and fakes, who raised their hands during every song and furiously wrote notes during every sermon. Who spoke words of encouragement, love and hope from the stage and then turned into spiteful devils the second their feet left the steps.

No more. God may exist, but he didn't love her...that was evident through the actions of his people as well as through all the trials he had thrown at her.

Yet Helen and Matthew stuck by her, inviting her over for supper or a movie. Keeping in touch and showing that they really cared. Because of them, Alex could not give up on the idea of God entirely – because there were two children of God who loved her. And through their acceptance she sometimes glimpsed the possibility of God loving her in the future.

Frans had made plans to spend a public holiday with Alex. She planned to go with her father to a hockey game in the morning and be dropped off at Frans's house on the way.

Alex had picked up a nasty cold, and was swimming in medication and a brain full of cotton. Setting her alarm on the 8th, she didn't notice that there was no small red dot in the top corner – that dot indicated that the time was in the morning. On the 9th her alarm did not go off, because it was set for the afternoon. Grant decided not to wake her because she was ill, when she eventually woke at midday there were several missed calls and texts on her phone from Frans. She called him immediately and told him what had happened, but he hung up. She called again and he didn't answer. She texted him and said she could still come for the rest of the day and he told her to forget it. She had ruined his plans, she always did that, she didn't care, they never talked, she never wore make-up, she never dressed nicely, she didn't care how he looked when they were together. Alex tried to explain things to him, but he was adamant that he was right.

Finally, when her airtime was nearly completed, they agreed to meet for dinner the next day and discuss things. Uneasily Alex slept, somehow knowing that the relationship she had tried so hard to hang on to, had died a long time before.

Dinner the next evening was tense, but they discussed many things. Alex promised the heavens and the earth – she would wear make-up and fancier clothes. She would walk every day and would never cut her hair. She would do anything he asked. Knowing they needed to talk more, Alex agreed to go back to Frans's house. No talking happened. He put on a movie and pushed himself inside her as if she was merely there for his pleasure. She was so dry it hurt, but she made her cry sound like a cry of pleasure. She just closed her eyes and focused on her breathing until it was over. Automatically she put him in her mouth and made sure he was happy. Then bruised and limping she went to bed.

For the rest of the month they didn't speak to each other. Each was too busy. Alex didn't want to go to his house anymore because she didn't want to be an object, but if he had summoned her she would have gone. Somewhere he must love her. Or at least she was doing something right to have kept him with her for so long. If she had to lie there every night for the rest of her life gathering bruises or sit there cramping her jaw muscles she would – because then she wouldn't be alone.

When her period failed to come at the end of August Alex knew what was happening. As secretly as she could she bought a pregnancy test kit and watched the faintest pink line appear. She showed her mother, who only said that Alex should phone the doctor on the Monday and see if there was enough blood left over from her iron test for a pregnancy test. Alex finally got hold of the doctor on Tuesday.

"Your iron levels are fine Alex, that's why I didn't call." The doctor told her

"Thank you doctor, but that's not why I am calling. I…I need to know if there is enough blood left over for a pregnancy test."

There was silence followed by a soft and sharp, "Oh." Alex closed her eyes and gripped the phone as if it was the key to survival. "Yes, yes there is. I will organise that now."

The next day, Wednesday, her doctor phoned with the news: Alex was indeed pregnant.

Karen was out on an errand when Alex's doctor phoned her with the news. Fear held her breath in its icy-hot grasp. Pregnant. Pregnant! The word seemed to become louder and louder until her ears were roaring and her whole core was filled with pure fear.

What would her father say? How angry would he be? Karen already knew – the test on the Saturday had been positive and this test was just a confirmation – but what on earth would her father say?

Shaking Alex picked up her phone and messaged Frans: *"You need to come over now please. I need to discuss something with you."*

A few minutes later her phone rang and Frans was on the other end of the line. Alex could hear wind in the background and knew he had crossed the street to the park where he could talk without his mother hearing.

"You're pregnant aren't you?" He demanded, apparently already knowing the answer

"Yes." She gave the monosyllabic answer that meant so much to her future.

"Fuck. Fuck, fuck, fuck, fuck, fuck…" He continued to repeat the word over and over and over. Alex swallowed and sat silently, waiting. Eventually Frans stopped swearing. "I'm coming over."

"Ok."

When he came Alex got into his car and they drove to the park. It had begun to rain, so they stayed in the car. Alex focused on counting the raindrops and joining them into patterns.

"What are you going to do?" He asked angrily

Those few raindrops over there made a star. "I'm going to keep the baby."

"Are you fucking insane? How will you afford to keep a baby? You family can barely afford to keep itself. Why keep a mistake?"

Over on the other side of the window there was a butterfly with dripping wings. "It's not a mistake. It is an accident."

"Same difference."

"Big difference." Silence fought with the falling of the rain as to what would make the loudest noise.

"You can't keep it. You have to get rid of it. What about me? It's not part of the plan to have a child now. I first have to get a job and then a house and then maybe get married. It's just cells. Get rid of it."

"It's not just cells." Alex closed her eyes and saw the image of the seal-like creature that the internet had shown her baby to look like at the moment. "It's a baby. It's my baby and I will not kill it."

"It's just cells. And you can't afford it. I can't afford it. You're being selfish." Frans hit the steering wheel. Realising he wasn't getting anywhere with this particular argument he switched tactics. "What about adoption?"

"No."

"Oh for Christ's sake why not!"

"Because I won't give up my child to be raised by someone else when I can raise it just as well. I will raise my child with all the love I have – it will know that it is loved and accepted and cared for. I will not abandon it."

"But you can't afford a child and it is not part of my plans! You are being so stubborn. You're not considering me at all."

Frans drove them back to Alex's house where they went inside and sat in silence. Karen came home and tried to mediate...but all that came out of that was that Frans would consider a relationship with Alex in the future if she wore make-up and fancier clothes and lost weight so she could look good on his arm in front of his friends. Knowing that further talk was a lost cause, Karen sent Frans home with instructions to come back the following night with his family for a discussion. He was also to come to Alex's doctor's appointment the next morning.

Alex sat in her room at her desk. Her phone pinged and blurrily she read a message from Helen inviting her over for dinner. Alex closed her eyes. She was even more of a sinner now than before – even less of a Christian. She would lose her friends. Wearily she responded: "I'm pregnant. If you still want me over I can come."

"See you at seven." The response came through.

So seven saw her sitting at the Swan's dining room table, where their son Sam had insisted that Alex sit next to him, and then after supper she had to play cars with him as they 'visited each other's houses' and got stuck in traffic jams. When it came time for bed he whispered something into his mother's ear and Alex heard Helen respond with, "Ask Alex."

"Alex, would you read me a story?" Sam's toe twirled against the floor and a book hung limply in his hand.

"Of course." She responded at the same time Helen said, "You don't have to if you don't want to."

Alex read Sam his story and then prayed with him before bed; a children's prayer of thanks for the day and help for good sleep and no monsters. Then she switched off his light and closed the door. Briefly pausing to gather some form of normality she made her way back to the lounge and helped Helen bath her youngest son, Mark, who had been born in January. After Helen put Mark to bed, she sat on the couch next to where Alex was sitting on the floor.

"What are you going to do?" Helen asked matter of factly, as though it weren't Alex's life she were talking about.

"I'm going to keep the baby."

There was no nod of approval, no shake of disapproval. Just peace and calm emanating from where Helen sat. Suddenly she got to her feet and went to the kitchen. Opening one of the cupboards she scratched for a bit and then returned, dropping a bottle of pills into Alex's lap.

"Folic acid. Take one each day. It's good for the baby."
Alex gripped the bottle as if it was a lifeline, her
knuckles as white as though she would never let go.
"You know I'm going to have to tell the pastor?"
Helen added, Alex nodded agreement, she had known
that would come. "What does Frans think?"

Alex finally burst forth with the conversation from
earlier. How he hadn't understood at all that it was not
a mistake. It was an accident, yes, but not a mistake. If
God had a plan for everybody, and if God never made
mistakes, then it couldn't be a mistake. If, like it had
been said, God had a purpose for her, then there was a
purpose for this child. But Frans was focussed on how
his plans had been messed up and how things were
now not in the order he had imagined them to be
unfolding.
"It's not a mistake, it's not." Alex just cried, tears
rolling down her face like rain rolling down a window.

All too soon her phone rang and her father was there
to fetch her. She stood and wiped her eyes. Taking a
breath she turned to thank Helen and was embraced by
the other woman. Alex knew that she must have
looked terrible, because Helen was not a 'huggy'
person, so a hug was something rare and special. As
she slipped into bed that night Alex realised something.
Helen had not rejected her.

The next day at her doctor's appointment the doctor
explained that she was pregnant and that there were
several options available to Frans and Alex. Alex sat in
silence and the doctor spoke about Abortion and
Adoption and keeping the baby. Finally the doctor
recommended counselling. On the way home Alex
contacted Jen, whom she had stopped seeing years
before when money had become too tight. Jen agreed
to a severely discounted rate and the first session was
set for the next morning.

That night the families met. Alex sat on one chair and
Frans on another, as far away from her as he could
possibly sit. His parents sat on one couch, Alex's
parents on their chairs. Frans did not say a word, not
even when his mother accused Alex of planning this.
Of not taking the birth control pills she should, or
taking antibiotics that would affect the birth control
and not telling Frans, or manipulating it some other
way. Frans said nothing. Eventually his dad looked at
Alex.

"What are you going to do?"

"I am going to keep the baby." She replied, the same
simple answer as always

"So basically you are using my son as a sperm donor."
He shot back

Alex's eyes began to fill with tears, she stiffened ready
for a fight. Blurrily she caught her father's eye and saw
his subtle hand movement telling her to keep calm and
silent. The meeting ended and they left. Frans still had
not said a word.

Therapy the next day was somewhat pointless. All that it served to do was cement the fact that each of them were set in what they wanted to do. Alex would not kill the baby. Frans would not keep it. A few more therapy sessions later Frans said that perhaps he would consider a relationship with Alex in the future, but not with the child. As hard as Alex tried to explain to him that one could not separate the two the more he refused to listen.

That night at her mom phoned during a tea-break from her work, she asked Alex if she and Frans had broken up. Whilst checking Facebook she had seen that he had changed his relationship status to single. Alex checked Facebook, and there staring her in the face was the fact that he had left. She realised that she would just have to do it on her own.

Alex knew that whatever the mother did affected the baby, and she tried so hard not to be stressed. She tried regulating her eating and actually eating three meals a day. She took the folic acid and the vitamins and listened to calming soothing music. Names took on new meanings, and she searched sites that she had previously only used to name characters in her books. Her father was supportive, as were the rest of her family. Yes, they could not afford another child, but they would make a plan.

In a vain attempt to settle the unrest between herself and Frans, she emailed him. He responded, she responded, and each response became more verbally and emotionally abusive until he finally 'uttered' the words: "I would have respected you more had you had an abortion because that's the type of woman I value." Alex was devastated, but she tried not to show it. She tried to stay calm for the baby. Even though medication also affects the child, she had to keep taking her psychiatric drugs in order for her to stay alive. And then one Saturday there were spots of blood in the toilet and her heart skipped several beats.

Panicked she phoned work and explained that she had to go to the doctor and couldn't come in, and her boss said that if she did not come to work on the Sunday she needn't bother coming in again.

There was nothing the doctor or nurses in the emergency room could do but try and calm her down. They advised her to raise her legs and try to relax, the best they could do was to schedule an appointment with the gynaecologist for the next morning. As her parents drove her to her appointment at the hospital that Sunday morning she bargained, prayed, begged and pleaded silently with her god. She would go to church again, she would forget how they had hurt her, she would raise her arms when she sang and she would listen to every sermon… just please let her baby be ok.

A tiny bean with a white speck showed on the screen. The white speck moved rhythmically. "Look at Beanie." Her mom said, and so her child had its nickname. Everything was ok and she could relax. As promised she went to church that morning and evening. It was uncomfortable and she felt as if she didn't belong, but she kept her word.

Two weeks later she had her next scan. Beanie was smaller than expected and the due date was pushed back. But the heartbeat was strong. Five days later Alex began to bleed, and there was more than just a few spots. She looked at the blood in her underwear and flushed cold. That night she lay with her legs up and her heart pounding. She knew. She tried to pretend it was ok, but her heart knew. The dog kept her company the whole night as if it knew too.

Driving to the hospital the next afternoon there was no bargaining or pleading, just a heavy silence. And when the doctor kept trying different angles without saying anything tears flowed without thought. Finally he spoke the dreaded phrase that burst her heart: "I can't find a heartbeat." 4 p.m. No heartbeat… Her bean was dead. God had taken a miracle and ripped it from her.

He had dangled love in front of her and then pulled it from her grasp. He had abandoned her again. She was alone.

She was hospitalised and had a D&C on the Tuesday morning. She was discharged the next morning and went home, straight to bed. She refused to eat, refused to drink, she felt as though her soul had died and left just her body unable to follow. She didn't leave her bed except to go to the bathroom.

Helen and their pastor visited that evening, and they all just sat there in silence. Alex was sure all she could feel was Helen's silent comfort and an air of disapproval and 'you got what you deserved' from the pastor. As they left, Helen hugged Alex.

For the next three months Alex only left her bed to go to the bathroom. She did not shower, she did not eat. She hardly slept but tried to sleep as much as she could just to make the days pass. Her mind kept trying to find that one thing she had done that had killed her baby. Was it the anti-depressants? Had they killed the baby? Had she stressed the foetus too much? Had she listened to the wrong music and caused an imbalance in something? Was it that paracetamol she had taken for her headache? What had she done that had killed her baby? Had she poisoned her body so badly with the overdose attempts and the bleach and the anti-depressants that it literally rejected the foetus? What had she done?

January 3rd came around and Alex could not stand it anymore. She took all the alcohol she could find in the cupboard and downed it. She spoke over the internet to her friend, saying goodbye, and her friend gathered together a whole lot of people who tried to support her. Random people she did not know came to her page on DeviantArt and left positive comments, comments of support, pleas for her to reconsider.

When everybody in the house was finally asleep at 5 a.m. Alex picked up her knife, said goodbye to her friend, and walked out of the house. She passed a patrolling police car and greeted them with a smile, blade hidden in her other hand. Steady and clear-headed, despite the alcohol, she reached the canal and went to sit under the bridge. Drawing the blade across her arm she opened up a large yellow eye that began to cry red into the dry stone below her. Again and again she drew the blade over the same cut, until her leg was soaked and the white sheep on her pyjamas had turned pink with embarrassment.

Sitting back against the wall, deflated and defeated, she closed her eyes, relaxed and uttered the first prayer in months: God, please let me die.

B y the time it had reached 6:30 a.m. she had not died and Alex realised that once more she was just a failure. Gathering the knife and house keys she walked disappointedly back home. A man on his way to work passed her and cheerfully said good morning, not noticing the blood that covered her as he went on his way.

The house was still when Alex let herself in and hung up the keys. She went to her computer and switched it on. Her friend was still online.

"It didn't work."

"Thank God!" The words appeared on her screen almost instantly. Alex quickly wrote a poem, the way that she expressed everything, about how God seemed to have listened to the pleas of strangers and kept her alive instead of listening to her and finally giving her peace. Then she walked into her parents' room and poked her mother awake. Karen jerked awake and blinked several times, trying to work out what was happening to wake her so suddenly.

"You should have listened to Helen." Alex murmured
to her

"Huh?"

"You should have listened to Helen." Alex repeated,
knowing that Helen had phoned her mother the night
before warning her that she suspected Alex would do
something. She bared her left arm and the cut that was
still oozing. There were two deep cuts accompanying
it, but that one was the main one.

"You told me you were fine." Karen shrieked, fear in
her voice as she sat up and simultaneously smacked her
husband on the head to wake him.

"What's happening?" Grant sat up rubbing his head.

"Her arm." Karen sat trembling. "What do you want
me to do Alex? What do you want me to do? I don't
know what to do anymore, I just don't." Tears slid
down her mother's cheeks and Alex felt as if she had
been punched in the gut. This was her fault. Her
mother was crying. It was her fault. She closed her eyes
and wished that she had just cut once more instead of
debating.

"I'm not taking you to the hospital," Karen stood up and began to pace, "I am not being lectured by incompetent know-it-all doctors who think they know the reasons behind everything when they have no idea what is going on. I am not getting lectured on how badly I've brought up my child." Alex swallowed. "And I'm certainly not having you lectured at as to how bad you are."

Her dad came with a paper towel and held it over the wound. Then he taped it there with masking tape. "Go lie down." He ordered

Alex did as she was told. She was numb, disappointed and just too tired. The very act of breathing exhausted her. She lay down for a while but did not sleep. She just lay there as if she was a rock in the sand and not a human who was breathing and alive.

"Get dressed." Her dad came into the room, giving her kindly orders as though she were a simpleton. "You are going to the doctor."

Alex dressed herself as best as she could single-handedly and followed her parents out the door. They drove to her doctor's offices, which were not officially opened yet. The doctor was there to meet them and they walked into her rooms. Karen sat on a chair while the doctor had Alex sat on the bed.

The doctor unwound the tape and removed the paper, which had stuck in the wounds. She examined the arm from different perspectives and then turned to Karen. "Two more millimetres and she would have succeeded."

Alex burst into tears inside, while outside she remained stoic and blank. Two millimetres? She was a failure because of two millimetres? Oh for fuck sake couldn't she do anything properly? She couldn't be a normal child; her body couldn't hold a child properly and she couldn't even kill herself properly.

"What do I do? What do we do?" Karen questioned.

"I'm going to stitch these up and then we call her psychiatrist. She needs to be admitted."

"But why? I don't understand why? What did I do wrong?" Karen wailed

Alex barely heard the words. She longed to tell her mother that she had done nothing wrong – Alex was just defective. She didn't work properly. She was ugly, worthless, pathetic, a failure, a murderer and she deserved to die. It had nothing to do with her mother. It was just her.

After stitching the wound and checking the mobility of her fingers her doctor phoned the psychiatrist.

"He's organising a bed for her." She said turning to Karen. "Take her home, pack, and he will call you when they can get her in. It will be today."

Alex went home and sat on her bed. She sent Helen a message, bluntly saying she had tried to kill herself and had failed and was going to the clinic. Helen came over to the house within a few moments and just sat with Alex. Even though she never asked, Alex found herself telling Helen what she had done, from the alcohol to the internet conversation, to the walk past the police and the way she had finally felt that it was going to be alright when she saw that blood trickling into the canal.

Helen briefly squeezed Alex's hand in a sympathetic and comforting manner to show her concern. "Let's pack your stuff." She offered quietly

Alex pulled clothes from the closet at random and stuffed them into the bag, along with some towels, toiletries, a book, her phone charger and other oddments she might need.
"No, let's pack properly." Helen smiled, taking everything out of the bag and folding things in such a

way that everything fit nicely and there was even extra space left over.

"You pack things like my dad. He is good at packing." Alex murmured

"I'm just maximising space and eliminating creases."

"Come. We're going." Helen and Alex turned to see Karen in the doorway. Peter carried Alex's bag and they trooped out the house. Helen said goodbye and promised to visit. Karen and Peter drove Alex to the clinic. She filled out admission forms and then waited for a nurse. The nurse asked questions and there were more forms to fill in, a declaration that she would not try hurt herself while in the clinic to be signed, and then she was shown to her room. Peter helped her unpack.

"Don't think we are going to come and visit you every day." Karen seemed to be speaking to the wall. "We can't afford the petrol. Don't expect us to visit." Alex concentrated on the towel she was folding. "And don't expect us to bring you things. We aren't going to come bring you things." Karen continued. Alex ignored her but was listening as she noticed the towel was cream in colour and had a hole in the one corner.

"Come Peter. Let's go." Karen gathered up her son in a whirlwind of motion and then they were gone. Alex sat on the bed as the brevity and reality still failed to sink in. She needed shampoo and toothpaste, but she couldn't ask her parents, they wouldn't bring her any. Her mother had just said so. She was alone with her depression and her thoughts, and the darkness inside of her swelled with pride. Then her phone pinged.

"Anything you need? Hope you are settling in." Helen. "I need shampoo and toothpaste but my mother just said that they won't bring me anything and they won't visit and she is really angry so I don't want to ask her. I'm settling in fine. I'm fine."

There was an announcement over the intercom about a group that was starting and Alex went down to the room. Intentionally or not the topic of the first group she attended was grief and loss. Alex listened to the occupational therapist explain some things during her

178

talk and the members were encouraged to share. Alex briefly shared an unemotional account of what had happened. Then they had to write a letter to the person, thing or part of themselves that had been lost. Alex could not bring herself to write a letter to Beanie, so she wrote to Frans. She let out her feelings of betrayal and confusion and anger. She told him what an ass and a jerk he was, how immature and stubborn and how he was so focussed on things going according to his plan that he hadn't planned for life. She wrote, but she did not cry. Emotionally numb she somehow managed to pour emotions onto a page – she had always been good at that.

Afterwards she went up to her room and just sat there on the bed. She picked up the book – a gift from Helen. "Where is God When it Hurts". She began to read.

The nurse came to remind her about supper and she went to the dining room, watching the other patients to see how the eating process worked. She got her meal and sat alone at a table. Some other patients joined her and introduced themselves. They tried to involve her in their conversation, but she just listened quietly. After supper they moved outside and sat there talking about things. Suddenly one of them looked at Alex.

"Do you suffer from Polycystic Ovarian Syndrome?" The stranger demanded as though from nowhere.

"Yes." Alex blinked; she wasn't sure what the others point was.

"Are you scared that the baby you lost was your only chance at a family?"

"Yes." Alex was too exhausted to pretend.

"It wasn't. Your little boy is in heaven now, but he wasn't your only chance." She looked up as her husband came through the gate and moved from the table. Alex sat trying to absorb what she had heard.

Alex thought back to December, when she had given Helen her Christmas gift. She had made a CD of herself playing some pieces on the piano because Helen had wanted to see a piano concert for her birthday but Matthew was not a classical music fan. In searching for pictures for the CD cover she had logged on to facebook for the first time in months. There had been a message from someone in the church in her inbox. The message said that the person had had a dream about Alex. In the dream Alex had been talking about a baby boy, but had not been happy about it as if something was wrong. Now this stranger had mentioned that her boy was in Heaven. The person from the church had not known about the pregnancy. Neither of them knew her struggle to lay to rest a faceless, nameless, genderless child – yet they had mentioned a boy, specifically.

That night Alex tossed and turned. Eventually she decided that perhaps God was apologising in his own way, but letting her know. So she named her son. James David. The names she had picked out long ago as what she would call her first-born son.

Alex spent three weeks in the clinic, learning different things in the occupational therapy groups. It was all beneficial and all of what she learned was interesting and helped her see some of the things that had been out of place. Her psychiatrist came every day and they worked on her medication. She was put on a mood stabiliser and an anti-psychotic…however she was never given a diagnosis. Her mother still insisted that she had some Bipolar traits, but the psychiatrist ignored her. He placed Alex on so much medication she walked like a zombie and her interactions were all through a sleepy haze.

Contrary to the words her mother had spoken, her family did visit. Helen visited, and one other member of the church. Other than that she was forgotten. Church body? Fellowship? Caring? Bullshit!

After her three weeks she still needed more treatment, but her medical aid only allowed for three weeks. Thus she went to the state facility. The groups there were mostly helpful, but not always so. She hated it. It was not beneficial at all. Getting out of there became her goal, and she played along to the best of her ability, becoming the model patient.

When she left they told her that she had Schizophrenia. They took her off the anti-depressants and gave her more anti-psychotics. Every Monday she had to attend a support group and once a month the doctor would see her to monitor her medication. After about six months of the support group she was told she only had to come in once a month to see the doctor.

Alex wasn't feeling any better. She was feeling worse. Her depression was clawing her insides to shreds and she was not sleeping at all. But she smiled and told the doctors that she was fine. The mask she wore convinced them, maybe because they had so many patients to care for, maybe because they simply believed her. They left her alone to take her meds even though they weren't doing anything.

Towards the end of August the year following the suicide attempt Alex sat in the doctor's room at the state facility and answered the questions fired at her with the same answers she always gave.

"How are you feeling?" The doctor would ask

"Really good." She would reply

"How do you think the medication is working?"

"Really well."

"Are you having any suicidal thoughts?"

"No, none at all."

The psychiatrist looked at Alex, and Alex took the opportunity to pose a question. "When can I start coming off these meds?"

"Well, the Lamotrogine you will be on for the rest of your life, but the Amytriptalene, Oxazapam and Risperdone we can decrease gradually." Alex felt relieved. "Let's take the Risperdone down from 4mg to 3mg." Alex blinked. "If that works for a few months then we can take it down again."

Alex sighed inwardly.

"You know, it was hard to diagnose you." Alex just looked on. "You were either a major depressive with psychotic symptoms or you were Schizophrenic. We eventually decided on Schizophrenic. See you next month."

Alex made the appointment and met her mother at the car.

"I'm not going back." She told her mother shortly

"Where else will you go?"

"I will find a private psychiatrist that my medical aid will pay for and go to them. I will not be diagnosed by the flip of a coin."

So she researched psychiatrists on her medical aid's approval list, and picked one. After one session with him he looked at her and told her she was not Schizophrenic. He immediately took her off all the medication except the Lamotrogine, and added the anti-depressant Fluoxetine. Then he asked her the question she knew he would ask.

"Are you feeling suicidal?"

"Yes." Alex closed her eyes and nodded, replying in a voice that was barely a whisper

After some phone calls and plans Alex was admitted back into the clinic September. The groups were the same topics as before, but Alex learned something new from each one. When she left she felt confident that she was on the right medication.

It took her medical aid two months to agree to pay for the medication, even though she now had a proper diagnosis of Major Depressive Disorder and Mild Bipolar Disorder. For those two months she had no medication because she simply could afford the thousands of Rands to purchase them. She held on as best as she could, and her friends held on with her.

She had many friends now – met through DeviantArt. People who also suffered from similar issues and were willing to share what had helped them. People that were willing to sit with her during nights from hell, people who would spend time just talking to her as she tried to rock herself into a comfort zone that was always out of reach.

Somehow a group of misfits, each suffering from a mental illness or some form of horror in their past, had formed a pack…and she was part of the pack. They looked after each other, and for the first time she felt that there would always be someone to turn to, no matter how far away they were.

Faceless people with hurts of their own placed those hurts in the background to help her up when she fell, and she did the same for them. Symbiotic, therapeutic – she was not alone.

October and May were hard months for Alex. Each October she relived the death of her son, and each May she remembered the day he should have been born. Christmas was particularly hard as there was a family lunch to attend.

The lunch was held by her aunt and uncle, and watching them act as a perfect family it was hard to imagine that her aunt wanted a divorce. Christmas was uneventful, but Alex's mind kept drifting to the Christmases she had experienced in the past. The times at her grandparents' house at the German Christmas time, events that would never be repeated again; her grandfather was dead and her grandmother was in a home for people with dementia. She wondered if her son would have enjoyed Christmas. Would have liked the toys or the wrappings best? They couldn't afford much, but they would have made it special for him.

Chatting to her friends that night she felt incredibly low. The desire to pick up the knife for the first time in a year was strong. And the desire to die was stronger. She chatted with her friends for a bit, tried to explain, then logged off. The next few days she spent in bed, and when she logged back on it was to frantic messages of 'where are you?' and 'are you ok?'

Despite her friends, Alex was desperately lonely. She longed to have someone who loved her. Someone she could love. Towards the end of January someone claimed to be that person, then dropped her after a week. Again she plummeted to the depths, only to be revived when he changed his mind. The next week however, he dropped her again and this time it was permanent.

The next month, after applying everywhere she could, she finally got a job. The title was office administrator, but she soon found herself doing personal work for her boss, like searching for bursaries for her daughter or phoning shopping centres and comparing their toilet paper prices. Any little mistake and her boss would explode, and then spend the rest of the day muttering behind her back. Alex needed the money for her family, so she worked more than her contracted hours. She did not take a lunch break or a tea break – not that she actually had one anyway. She now had a job, and despite the pressure from her boss she could do it and did it well as the required tasks were well below her intelligence level. Of her own accord she created a company website, which her boss took great pride in boasting about as if it had been her idea. She worked hard and stressed over money and losing the job – for she was only supposed to be part-time. Then her boss re-opened another company she had founded and Alex was switched to that side of things. However, it was going slowly and soon her boss was moaning that she was costing this company money because it wasn't generating money yet she had to be paid at the end of the month. Alex had to put up with the fear of being fired, the constant mood changes of her boss, being blamed for her boss's mistakes and hearing the bad talk about her colleague when her colleague was off sick.

Her boss was belittling, condescending, rude, negative, and often, treated Alex as if Alex was of a lower intelligence level than she actually was, simply because she, herself, was not as good at writing or English, or had computer skills at the level Alex possessed. Yet every time she needed to word a formal email it was to Alex that she turned with a beautiful smile as if nothing was wrong at all.

Still lonely, at the advice of a friend she joined an online dating site, and got many responses from people who had only looked at the photo of her face and not read a single word she had written in her profile. One man claimed to have read the profile, so she met him for coffee. He told her stories about how badly he had been treated by the people of Cape Town and how he was just looking for someone beautiful like her.

The next week she sent him a message instead of phoning him, and he exploded with anger saying that he was not showing that she loved him. She was arrogant, if she ever hoped to get a guy her attitude needed to change. Meekly she agreed to phone him each day. May first, a public holiday, he came over to her place to watch a movie. Desperate for love she gave in to the pressure of his argument that if she loved him she would allow him to have sex with her. Again she found herself lying legs spread and dry while someone grunted above her and bruised her in haste and selfishness.

Her mind screamed that it was wrong, it felt wrong, she knew him but not well enough. She liked him but not that much. Still her head ruled and she gave in to keep someone by her side, desperate for someone to love her.

Mid May there was a large argument with the friend who had helped her before. That girl had basically accused a mutual friend of being responsible for his autism and depression. When Alex stood up for the person, her 'friend' wrote her a nasty Facebook message about how nobody would look twice at her ugly body but maybe if she got someone drunk enough they would give her a good fuck and hopefully the baby wouldn't die. Alex was shaken. She hadn't deserved that. The next day she took 40 paracetamol tablets to work and swallowed them at lunch time. Then she went back to work, just a little bit woozy. Her internet friends knew, and one of them had her parent's email address.

"Has your father discussed the email with you?" Karen stood in the doorway and Alex turned from the computer.

"What email?"

"The one from one of your friends. Where he says that you took an overdose and he is worried about your liver."

"It hasn't been discussed no."

"How many tablets did you take?"

"About 40."

"When did you take them?"

"Thursday at work."

"Why didn't you tell me or phone your psychiatrist? That is what he is there for."

"I didn't think of it at the time. I just hurt. I was trying to cope with May and then this thing happened and I couldn't cope."

"You shouldn't have let her get to you. You are better than her and you know it."

"I know."

"We need to find some way of getting you through May and October."

"And Christmas."

Karen blinked then nodded. "And Christmas. Next time, talk to me or your doctor." She walked out of the room and Alex went back to the computer.

Alex spent so much time stressing about her work, that when she caught flu and her doctor booked her off she ignored her doctor and went to work anyway. Through the internet site she met a wonderful man who understood her and they could sit talk for hours. After their first meeting they both felt whole. July first he asked her out, and she said yes. Still she overworked and stressed. She had gone back to not eating, which did not help the fact that she was now diabetic. Diagnosed with hypertension, stressing over work and working so hard was not helping at all. She could not shake the flu, and every time she visited her doctor her blood pressure was higher than the time before. Eventually she was admitted to hospital to control the blood pressure and flu. After a week of painkillers that could not cure the headache she had possessed for the last three months Alex began having panic attacks. She was definitely going to lose her job, and what about the money? What would the family do? Would she be able to find another job? Her boyfriend had been fired mid-July and was also searching for a job, yet most days he visited her in hospital and just sat there talking with her and trying to get her to stop stressing. On her final night in hospital her psychiatrist came to see her. "What happened to you? You were doing so well the last time I saw you." He asked

"I have this pressure in my neck, which leads to my head and brings about headaches so bad I have to take six Myprodol at once and lie down. I am shaking worse than before and I think I am starting to have panic attacks."

The following day she went straight from hospital into a different clinic. After a conversation with her psychiatrist, he upped her medication to the level it used to be – even though he had halved it only two weeks prior.

Alex didn't know if this clinic would work, but she was determined to try. She had to get her life right. Get a job, or keep the one she had, control her depression and bipolar, as well as the anxiety she now had, the agoraphobia, the social phobia and the slight traces of OCD and PTSD. She was unsure of her diagnoses, but hoped that by the end of the three weeks that would be clear and she could work with it instead of having it work against her.

The medication, her family, the doctor and her boyfriend were there to support and help her heal. She finally realised that she could not do this alone. She could not fight this fight without a companion and could not even hope to survive without the support structure that had been there all the time if she had only thought to look for it.

She was not alone, she did not have to be alone. She could not fight this alone, and she did not have to.

E ach person enters a clinic for a different reason and with different problems, but every person has something in common – they have problems and are trying to face them and beat them or learn skills that will help them cope with the problems in the future.

For Alex being in a clinic, even though it was the third time, was no shame. It was an opportunity to maybe finally put her demons to rest. To understand the darkness that had been with her since she was little and finally be able to confine and cage it. And, if not cage it, perhaps release it so that it no longer consumed her heart and overwhelmed her.

With hindsight, Alex realised that had she not been terrified of being labelled with the word 'depression' all those years ago she would have had help much sooner and many things would not have happened. There might have been less suicide attempts, maybe the right medication would have been found sooner and she would be living a normal life.

At 26 she was finally realising that the scared little girl still existed inside of her. The person petrified of being abandoned and rejected, of being unloved and unlovable. A little girl with her own set of problems that would be dealt with eventually with the help of an extremely kind psychologist. At the same time she realised that there were truths she knew that kept that fear in check most days. She knew her boyfriend loved and supported her. She knew her family would be there when she needed them. She was beginning to trust that perhaps the right medication would be found. She was no longer entirely afraid of the stigmas attached to the words 'depression', 'bipolar' or the word 'schizophrenic'. Being one, or more, of those things did not make her less of a person. It was simply an illness that she couldn't help having. She had not chosen it. It had been born with her. Had she realised this sooner perhaps her life would have taken a different path and she would be a qualified teacher making her dreams come true.

However, she would not go back and change her choices. They had made her into the person she was. Her choices had made her the woman with the big heart who would give everything to help someone in trouble. Made her the person who knew how it felt to be depressed, bipolar, anxious, confused and alone. She was the girl who had flirted with anorexia and bulimia and knew their dangers. She was the soul that had gone through a miscarriage and all that entailed. True her choices had also made her become the disillusioned Christian who realised the fakes that filled the religious systems but there was still something in her that believed, because of two people. All of those things allowed her to help others who were like her. New friends she met online who needed encouragement. Who felt like dying and needed a conversation to calm them. Who struggled with cutting and just needed to know that it could be beaten – that there was a possibility that they too could beat something they thought impossible to stop.

It was a long journey, and she knew there was still a long way to go, but she also knew that whatever happened she had the support she needed to survive. She still had a lot to learn; how to manage her anxiety and fear of crowds, how to pull herself out of her head when the depression set in, how to calm herself when the bipolar took her bouncing into a cleaning spree and then vanished to leave her flat and empty upon the bed. To learn those things would take time, medication, training…help.

Alex found help at the clinic. More help than she had ever received in her life. Within a day it came out that the death of her son was a hurt that she was holding in her heart and that she had not let go of. She would always be stuck in the hurt and depression cycle if she could not move on – but wouldn't that mean that she would forget him?

The hardest thing Alex had to accept at this stage was not that she suffered from mental illness, but that she needed help and could not manage it on her own. She needed to lean on people sometimes. She didn't have to pretend to be strong when she wasn't, and she didn't have to wear a mask and say she was fine when she was really falling apart. This was particularly hard in front of a group of strangers in a clinic, even though she knew that each one was there for a reason. When she could no longer hold the pain inside and broke down in tears in front of the group she found herself surrounded by bodies hugging her and patting or rubbing her shoulder. Words were whispered in her ears. "Let it out, it's ok." "Just let it out, don't bottle it up." Some tissues magically appeared in her hands and after a while she stopped shaking and sobbing. The facilitator of the group turned to her and asked her how she felt.

Alex hated crying. To her it was a sign of weakness. She answered the counsellor with the truth. "I feel ashamed." The group assured her that there was nothing to be ashamed of and when the group ended Alex sat with the nurse in charge until she was ready to stand and go to her room. That night she made sure that she ate either before or after everybody else just in case they were secretly judging her.

The following day, during a session with the same counsellor, he asked the group to share their greatest fear. One of the members broke down as she re-lived the death of her mother, and it was Alex's turn to comfort. She wrapped her arms around the woman and placed her head on the woman's shoulder. Her hand found the woman's and was squeezed as the memory continued to its completion – as if the person was drawing strength from Alex. It took Alex a while to realise that she had been doing just that – drawing strength from someone kind enough to offer comfort when it was needed most, even though they may not be strong themselves.

Two days later the group was talking about how they felt and one member shared a deep tragedy that had happened to her. She began sobbing and Alex and the others came to give her comfort. The counsellor kept saying "beautiful, beautiful, let it all out" while the other members asked gentle questions that only Alex could hear. After comforting the woman, Alex sat back exhausted. Tears trickled from her eyes. The woman had spoken about a memorial service she had attended, and Alex realised that she had not had a memorial for her son. She had gone on with her life simultaneously remembering him and trying to forget that he existed. Tears trickled down her face and the group comforted her. The same woman as before whispered words of comfort to her.

"It was not your fault." "You gave him what you could." After the hugging and crying was over the counsellor praised everyone for feeling free to share their emotions as well as to comfort each other – part of the support system in the clinic. He briefly spoke about memorial services and something switched in Alex's brain – what if she had a memorial for her son?

That weekend she planned it. One of her greatest sorrows was that there was neither tombstone nor box of ashes she could periodically visit and pay her respects. The only thing she could think of that would be able to help remind her was a tattoo. She phoned a tattoo parlour and the receptionist gave a hesitant guess at a cost of about R1700. Alex's heart sagged – there was no way her family could afford that. Be that as it may she still phoned her mother and asked, knowing the answer before the outcome. Surprisingly her mother, who had told her that tattoos were only for sailors and thugs, was not opposed to the idea but actually welcomed it. After discussing the impossibility of the cost there was a voice in the background. "Peter says he has a friend who owns a tattoo place. He will ask his friend if he will do it at a discount."

By the time supper came around Alex had found out the cost: R600. That, although still more than her family could afford, was more feasible. She did not have a design in mind, because she couldn't visualise one, but all she knew was that she wanted a heart with wings and her son's name inside…and that it mustn't look animated or like clip art. Alex contacted her boss and asked for her salary – even though she had spent almost the entire month in hospital and then the clinic. Discussing with a fellow patient, Alex wondered about her salary. It was normally used to cover her medical aid, which cost about R600. If the salary came to R600 she would sacrifice the tattoo for the medical aid. The other patient said that in all honesty she would probably do the same.

At one o'clock the next morning her boss sent a message through: "You've worked eight days, your salary is R1200." Alex looked at that number in shock – enough to cover both the tattoo and medical aid.

Perhaps God was giving her a sign, giving her 'permission' to let her son go so that he could finally be the best angel he could be. Enough money for both things, not a rand more or a rand less, just enough. The next day Alex, Peter and Grant went to Peter's friend's tattoo parlour. Alex asked for a pen because the one she used to sign her permission documents was a nice one, and he gave her one straight from the box. Then a short girl with some amazing tattoos came through with a sketch. It was beautiful. The heart and the wings and the name all fit perfectly and looked stunning.

"Do you like it?" The girl asked

"It's stunning."

"What colours were you imagining?"

"Red heart, white wings, black name."

"Not at all what I pictured."

"What did you picture?" Alex asked nervously, wondering if another dream was about to be dashed.

"A heart that goes slightly shaded up to a bit of pink, some blue and white on the wings…"She continued speaking but Alex had tuned her out. She just couldn't picture what was being described to her, yet at the same time she could. "So, what do you think?" The tattoo artist was bouncing on the balls of her feet. "Your way. Your colours, everything. It sounds amazing."

Alex spent an hour getting the tattoo done and sitting in that chair was the most relaxed she had felt in three months. She closed her eyes and nearly fell asleep as every muscle in her body calmed down with the beat of a heart connected to a brain saying that this was the right thing to do.

Monday Alex discussed the memorial she had planned with the counsellor and it was planned for Friday at two o'clock. She shared her plan with the group, and as they offered suggestions she was grateful that she was not alone in the planning process. One member offered to do the technical side as far as the songs were concerned because she shouldn't and couldn't be worrying about that while she was focussed on the memorial. That same man offered the suggestion of buying a helium balloon and just releasing it after the service as a final act of letting go of the hurt that had consumed her for so long. Not forgetting her son, but finally becoming at peace with his death and letting all the pain go.

The past would always haunt her, but there was a possibility of a future. It is said that when God closes a door he opens a window. So many doors had closed in Alex's face that she had turned her back and just given up. However, it seems that God had not given up on her. He opened a window and when she climbed through she found the most amazing man in the world. Her fairy prince who would help Thumbelina grow her wings. She also found a clinic full of people who were supporting and kind and who accepted the things she was suffering from and were helping her deal with them.

God had not forgotten her…and maybe, just maybe, despite the actions of his people, he loved her.

With the the possibility of love from God, Alex could see the love of her family that had been there the whole time. They may not have understood, but they had always loved.

The day of the memorial arrived. As she had asked for all that was there were some candles and a single red rose placed near the only pictures she had of him; two sonograms. Even though those were the only images she had, she was grateful that she had them.

The service started and Alex vowed that she would never cry. However, listening to the songs that her family had picked out for her, as well as the lyrics she read as an opening to her eulogy, her heart finally won a battle over her brain and she started crying. Half-way through the eulogy she could no longer see the words she was reading and had to blink several times before she could continue. More songs followed, and then

Karen said a few words. Alex cried at the emotion and love that came from her mother. She could feel the acceptance and understanding, but most of all the love.

At the end of the memorial Alex felt calm and peaceful about that particular part of her life. She had let the hurt go. Peter and her father left for another appointment, and as they left Peter gave her a big strong hug. Alex was shocked – Peter was the typical 'cowboys don't cry' man and barely showed emotion. Yet he had hugged her tightly and she had felt protected and safe.

Before the cake and tea Alex took the two blue helium balloons with James's name on them and the group walked outside into sunshine that had been rain not half an hour before – another blessing from God to show he was there. It was difficult to let go of the balloons, but as she felt the ribbons slip through her slowly relaxing fingers she felt a huge weight lift off her shoulders. All that hurt and pain she had been holding onto for all those years was gone.

She was not alone, and never would be again. There was her boyfriend, her family, her friends – all part of her support structure. Through the clinic's life skills programme with the occupational therapist she was learning to treat herself the way she treated others, talk to herself the way she would talk to others, affirm herself the way she affirmed others. She had not overcome all her issues, but the one she had overcome had freed her from the bondage of that hurt she had carried and harboured for all those years.

Before she had faced her issues alone, and failed, but now she would face them with a strong support structure and the newly-learned ability to look into the future with a possibility of a future. A newly-learned ability to think positively and believe in herself – as is written in the Bible: "For I know the plans I have for you. Plans for a hope and a future."

Going to the clinic where she was forced to face her issues was exactly what she had needed. Looking at things from a new perspective opened up many possibilities of a productive future.

She had overcome some of her main obstacles with the help of those who were there if she asked, and did not run away when she asked. She now had a future to look forward to...

The Greatest Fight of Your Life
15-8-13

It's a never-ending trial of fire,
To live together with a mind
Twisted by Depression's grasp
And by its claws refined.

Just when you think it's over
And you can finally see the sun,
The clouds come pouring over
And you realise you've just begun.
Looking back with hindsight
You can see how far you've come,
But the road ahead is rocky,
And it's a road that must be run.

Most obstacles are yours alone
To overcome and face,
You cannot pass the baton
Or put another in your place.

When you've hit a blockage
And you cannot breech the wall,
Though you've tried all your trusted tricks
They haven't worked at all,
Perhaps an evaluation's due,
A search for whom to call
When your tether's reached its tether
And you're heading for a fall.

The hardest part to darkness
Is believing in the light,
And that fighting for your mind and soul
Is a fight that's worth the fight.

214

About the Author

Joanne Bolton has lived in Cape Town, South Africa, all her life. She loves her 'mother city' but hopes to travel one day; a longing instilled into her by a History teacher and his explanations of museums and palaces in foreign lands.

www.ingramcontent.com/pod-product-compliance
Lightning Source LLC
Chambersburg PA
CBHW071423090426
42737CB00011B/1551